• HALSGROVE DISCOVER SERIES ➤

AGATHA CHRISTIE'S DEVON

Bret Hawthorne

HALSGROVE

First published in Great Britain in 2009
Reprinted 2010, 2017 and 2023

Copyright © Bret Hawthorne 2009

All rights reserved. No part of this publication may be reproduced,
stored in a retrieval system, or transmitted in any form or by any
means without the prior permission of the copyright holder.

British Library Cataloguing-in-Publication Data
A CIP record for this title is available from the British Library

ISBN 978 1 84114 856 4

HALSGROVE
Halsgrove House,
Ryelands Business Park,
Bagley Road, Wellington, Somerset TA21 9PZ
Tel: 01823 653777   Fax: 01823 216796
email: sales@halsgrove.com

Part of the Halsgrove group of companies
Information on all Halsgrove titles is available at: www.halsgrove.com

Printed and bound in India by Parksons Graphics

CONTENTS

Maps	4
Introduction	5
1 Greenway House & Garden, The Battery, The Boathouse	6
2 Ashfield	19
3 All Saints	25
4 The Princess Pier	30
5 Beacon Cove	34
6 Meadfoot Beach	38
7 Cockington	44
8 Anstey's Cove	49
9 The Pavilion	54
10 The Grand Hotel	60
11 Torquay Hospital	64
12 The Moorland Hotel, Haytor, Dartmoor	69
13 Kents Cavern	77
14 Sittaford Tor, Chagford	82
15 The Imperial Hotel	87
16 Churston Station	94
17 Elbury Cove	99
18 The Princess Gardens	104
19 Burgh island	108
20 Dartmouth, The River Dart and Royal Castle Hotel	116
21 Dittisham and Galmpton	124
22 Salcombe	130
23 Churston Church and Court	134
24 Blackpool Sands	139
Appendices	142

THE SOUTH HAMS & DARTMOOR
DARTMOOR
Totnes
Torbay
Modbury
KINGSBRIDGE
Start Bay
Bigbury Bay
Start Point
N
W
E
S
Key
1 Greenway
2 The Moorland Hotel, Haytor
3 Sittaford Tor (Chagford)
4 Churston Station
5 Elbury Cove
6 Burgh Island
7 Dartmouth
8 Dittisham
9 Salcombe
10 Churston Church
11 Blackpool Sands

MAP OF TORQUAY
St Marychurch
Shiphay
Babbacombe
Cockington
TORQUAY
N
W
E
S
Key
1 Ashfield
2 All Saint's Church
3 Princess Pier
4 Beacon Cove
5 Meadfoot Beach
6 Cockington
7 Anstey's Cove
8 The Pavillion
9 The Grand Hotel
10 Torquay Hospital
11 Kent's Cavern
12 The Imperial Hotel
13 Princess Gardens

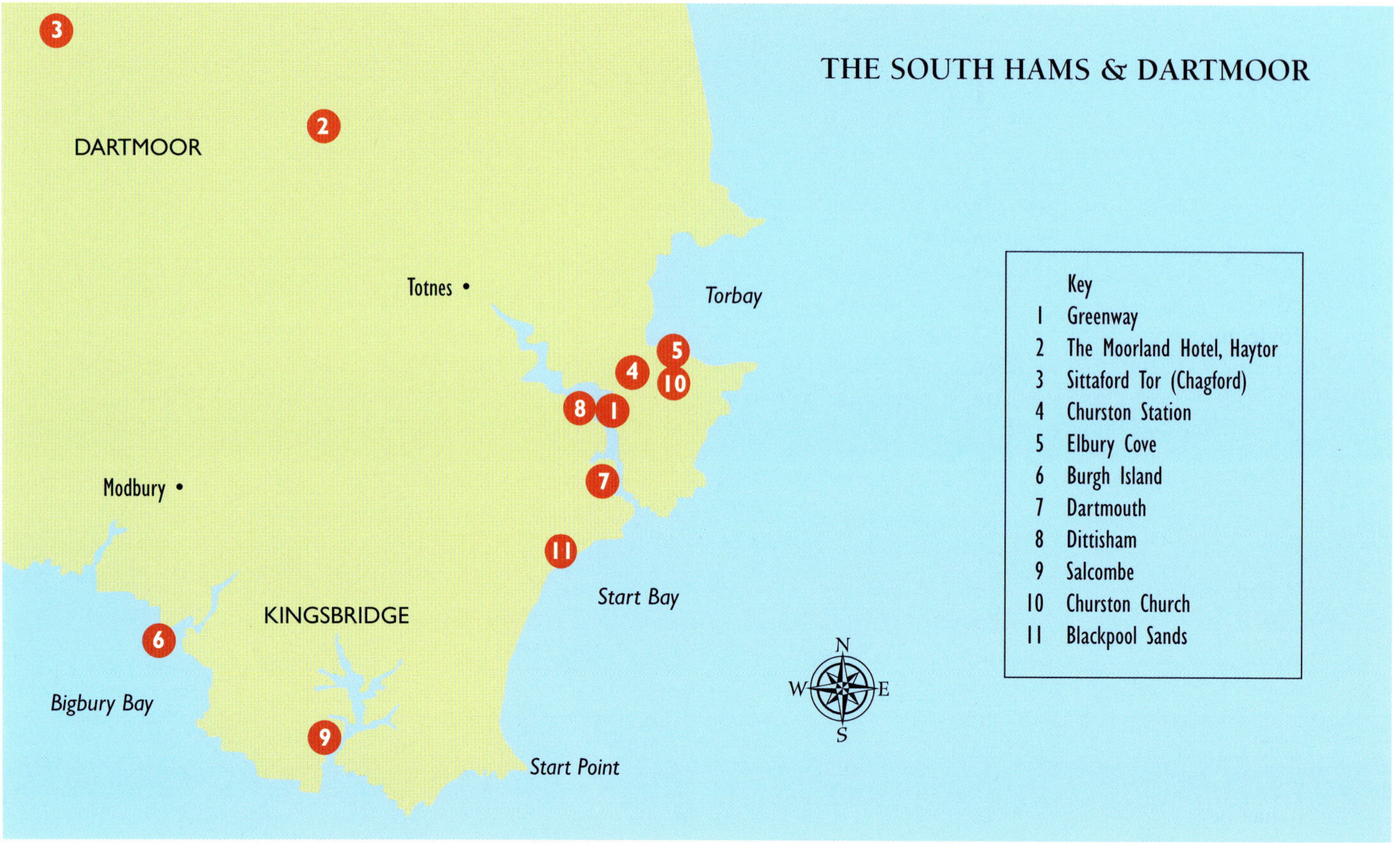

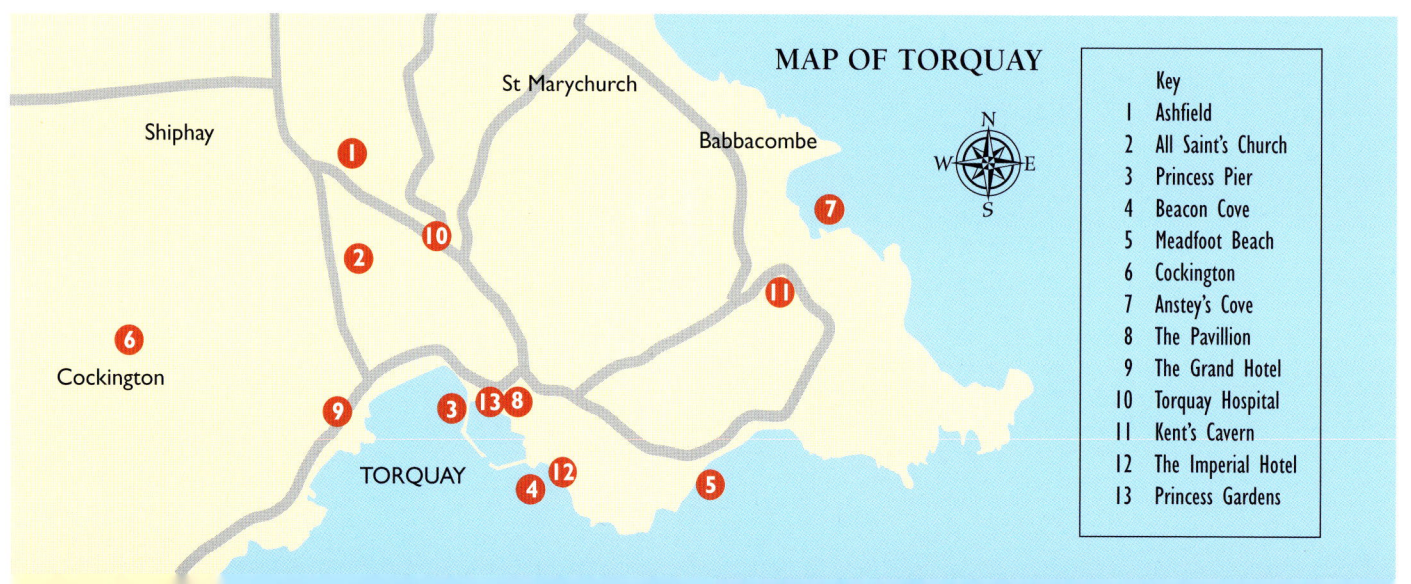

INTRODUCTION

Serendipity, they call it. Summer 2007 - a chance excursion with my new family to Greenway, a name I'd heard of on many occasions but just never got round to visiting. And the first time I'd picked up a camera in almost 20 years.

As for detective stories, I'd been reading them for as long as I could remember – Wilkie Collins, Conan Doyle and more recently P D James, Patricia Cornwell, Minette Walters, and the Swedish writer, Henning Mankell. But for sheer variety and ingenuity of plots, Agatha Christie still stood out from the rest. It's the detective story in its purest, most classical form. Agatha Christie is the Mozart of crime writers.

My photos came out well. One, in particular, of The Battery, gave me an idea. I remembered that several of the novels had been set in South Devon – I recalled a description of Elbury from *The ABC Murders* and hadn't an artist character met his end (in mysterious circumstances of course), precisely here, overlooking the river?

What I had in mind was a book for Christie fans like myself. A book that clearly showed the locations used in the novels. Simon Butler, at Halsgrove, put me on the right track. If you are going to write about the locations of Agatha Christie's novels why not also tell the story of what writing this book meant to you; what did you find out, how did you go about it, and how did that make you feel? Let the readers in on your own personal detective story as you discover the mysteries of Agatha Christie's Devon. Have the courage (I was probably unconsciously shying away from this) to find your own voice.

And it has been a voyage of discovery. Discovering the unrivalled beauty of the Devon that Agatha Christie loved so much, discovering the fascinating history and characters that lie behind it. All the while meeting the friendliest of people, and all the while getting just that little bit closer to the enigmatic personality of the most famous crime writer ever. I think, too, I found out quite a lot about myself along the way.

The maps opposite show the places I visited. At the end of the book there is a list of the novels referred to in the various chapters. Each of the chapter-locations stands alone – you can pick and choose as many or as few as you wish.

Happy hunting!

Bret Hawthorne
Paignton, January 2009.

1
GREENWAY HOUSE & GARDEN, THE BATTERY, THE BOATHOUSE

The Jewel of the Dart

Dead Man's Folly, 5 Little Pigs

Magnolias, rhododendrons and camellias

Are you the sort of person who cringes when the garden makeover guy decides to cover the whole lot with slabs? Is the mere mention of bark chippings anathema to you? Have you ever rushed out after an hour with Diarmuid Gavin and bought yourself a tree fern? If so, you will love Greenway.

The horticultural cognoscenti amongst you will understand when I say that Greenway is a plantsman's, not a gardener's, garden. Plants, flowers, shrubs and trees are not subsumed here into an over-arching design. They are the protagonists – and luxuriant, unbridled, unfettered protagonists they are too. The guests at Ariadne Oliver's fete in *Dead Man's Folly* did not all share my point of view – they lament the lack of nice flowerbeds and the fact that there are only trees and more trees. They were, quite simply, wrong.

The drive gives a taste of things to come. Giant sequoias soar skywards; there are palms, rhododendrons, camellias and azaleas bursting forth on all sides. One camellia catches the eye; the flowers of such a deep, dark blood red you almost expect them to start dripping in front of you. The retaining walls of the garden are bulging as if struggling to contain their tenants; flying buttresses strain to support them.

Agatha Christie had visited Greenway as a child with her mother, who had thought it the most perfect of the properties on the Dart. She, too, considered the white Georgian house with its fine shrubs and trees sweeping down to the river almost a dream come true.

The path turns left towards the house. We are approaching the spot where Ariadne placed the second clue in her ill-fated murder mystery. Through an arch in the wall, there's a glimpse of a solitary, brick-red tennis court surrounded by twisted, contorted magnolias. For a tennis

(Left) *Anyone for tennis?*

(Right) *The Vinery*

buff like myself this garden is already approaching paradise. What more could one ask for? A set, a shower, cocktails, dinner, then a leisurely stroll down to the river with a glass of champagne to watch the dusk draw in...

The tour of the garden starts through another arched gateway. There is a rectangular lawn with a pretty greenhouse, the Vinery, against the wall on the left. I have seen photos of a magnificent lilac waterfall of wisteria cascading down this wall, but not today.

Leaving the Vinery and its giant purple-leaved banana behind, the first specimen that catches the attention is a *Colletia paradoxa* – an amazing shrub with the wickedest spines imaginable – a natural forerunner to the modern military's most sadistic forms of barbed wire. It is easy to see why it is sometimes called the Crucifixion Thorn. Native to South America, it would make perfect hedging material for those with problems with intrusive neighbours.

On the left of the arch leading out of the garden is *Rosa bracteata*, known as the McCartney rose, prized by hybridists for its natural resistance to disease. In late summer it sports beautiful large white flowers with a central mass of golden-orange stamens. The scent has been described

AGATHA CHRISTIE'S DEVON

Colletia paradoxa - *The Crucifixion Thorn*

(Right) Rosa bracteata - *The McCartney Rose*

(Below) The Fernery

as lemon, apricot, even acetone. It thrives well with most bed-fellows – except perhaps heather.

The Fernery was a fashionable feature introduced by owners in the Victorian period. The air is cool, shady and damp with a central fountain surrounded by fronds and a flight of steps leading to nowhere. Set above the rockery are the headstones of departed pets. Agatha Christie's voice sounded very much like Her Majesty and she also shared her passion for small dogs – one actually playing a starring role in her last novel, *The Postern of Fate*. The overly precise ages recorded for these late companions is touching evidence of the affection they enjoyed.

The right-hand path leads back to the lawn, the left takes you along a box-hedge lined path where Ariadne's final clue – the key to the boathouse – was concealed. It has beds of cyclamens, wild strawberries or hydrangeas, depending on the season.

This is part of the magic of Greenway: the same tour at an interval of a couple of months is a totally different experience. Add to this is a network of criss-crossing paths and the garden has as many different permutations in space and time as a novel by Cortazar. Poirot, himself, complains that he finds the paths confusing.

There are other strange things going on in the garden too: there is the 'Bob Hope' camellia which I saw on one occasion but have never seen since; there is a beautiful blue tree that I photographed looking up from the boathouse one day and which has apparently now completely vanished; there is said to be a mother and child sculpture somewhere which I have never been able to find.

Departed friends

The first view of the house

(Left) A strategically placed bench

(Below) A glimpse of the river

Now to the right there is a giant araucaria which would have reminded Agatha of Ashfield – she makes particular mention of it in her autobiography. A bank of acanthus lies beyond, and farther still comes your first view of the house, the white façade squarely planted to look out over the river.

The path inclines gently upwards towards the Top Garden. On one visit I stop to sit on a bench. I had imagined these were placed strategically to allow the less fit among us to catch their breath. I now realise that they have also been perfectly sited to afford the best vistas down to the river.

AGATHA CHRISTIE'S DEVON

The view towards Dartmouth

(Opposite page) A vision of Eden

The hot garden, known as the Top Garden.

Spires and spikes

This is the other magic of the place: its stupendous location. On a hot day the river shimmers blue through the trees in the sunshine. From below there is a constant drone of pleasure boats, occasionally the rhythmic thumping of a steam train. But it doesn't disturb – it is 'out there' in the real world and we are here, cocooned in this latter-day Garden of Eden.

Continuing towards the top corner, tree cover stops and the temperature rises perceptibly. Spires and spikes predominate and the air is heavy with the cloying perfume of curry and clematis. The view down towards the river is spectacular.

And then down again into the shade. If you ever wondered what your *Pieris japonica* or *Dickinsonia antarctica* would get up to if freed from their containers; or what your spindly potted *Phyllostachys nigras* would achieve when left to its own devices, then you will discover as you descend steeply towards the river.

The garden near the house, within the walls, is fairly restrained. Beyond them the principle of entropy kicks in. The further one moves from the house, the more the element of chaos takes over. Even Poirot, the lover of all things logical and neat, could not help but admire the wild beauty of the place.

What I remember most about my walk around the garden with Nick Haworth, Assistant Head Gardener, is his story of Antony Hicks' deep interest in Eastern philosophy. He was a great believer in the Japanese concept of Wabi Sabi. It is all about discovering beauty in the impermanence of things; realising that things are beautiful because of their imperfections – everything changes and passes and we should embrace that transience. Anthony wanted to

(Left) The Bird Pond

(Centre) A British woodland – the Middle Path

(Right) White narcissi against birch

Narcissi among ferns

create a garden which, without being completely wild, was the memory of something that had gone before.

At the foot of the slope is the Bird Pond, with a headless bird statue by Bridget McCrum and masses of delicate purple iris and gunnera – gigantic spiky rhubarb. There are electric blue damsel flies hovering and darting just above the surface of the water lilies in an elaborate mating dance. At this time of the year – May – the sides and shallow sunlit spaces are black with tadpoles, their back legs well-developed and their tails already beginning to shrink.

Continuing along the Middle Path you have the part of the garden which most resembles an idyllic British woodland. Depending on the time of year, you will find vast swathes of yellow and white narcissi, primroses, bluebells or foxgloves. A zig-zag path once led up back to the high garden from here.

Now visitors can take the path leading down and away from the house where they will pass the secluded pond presided over by the Japanese Goddess of Mercy, Kwan Yin, set back and surrounded by dense vegetation.

At the lowest corner of the garden there is a fine view again down the Dart past the boatyards to Kingswear and Dartmouth. The path then turns back towards the Boathouse.

The Boathouse

It's a slightly misleading name. The main section in fact houses an outdoor sitting room complete with fireplace, sofas and balcony overhanging the river. In *Dead Man's Folly*, Greenway becomes Nasse House (presumably suggested by Noss Creek just downstream from the estate). In the novel, it is here that Mrs Oliver and Hercule Poirot visit Marlene who has volunteered to play the victim in the Murder Mystery devised for the fête at the house. Unfortunately, fiction has become reality and Poirot can only confirm the death of the girl. The basket chair that the horrified Mrs Oliver slumps into is still there. The magazines are still there too, their pages rustling gently in the breeze. For a Christie fan, this is as good as it gets.

By tradition, the boathouse at Greenway is where Sir Walter Raleigh, freshly returned from the New World and calmly sucking on his pipe of tobacco, was liberally doused with a flagon of ale by a servant who believed he had caught fire.

The Boathouse from downriver

The Boathouse at high tide

Below the boathouse is a plunge pool where one could bathe in seawater: it's still possible at high tide. It had become fashionable with the health-conscious after George III had set the example by 'taking the waters' at Weymouth (a similar bathing station is to be seen at Elbury Cove). The door to the pool has a sign warning that only those in possession of a bat licence may enter. The protection of horseshoe bats is undoubtedly a serious business but one cannot help but smile as childhood memories of Gotham City return to mind.

The air inside is cold and dank; the water dark, murky and totally uninviting. In such a place one can only conclude that: 1. it is a good thing that fashions have changed and we now swim in the sun and the open air and 2. if George III championed bathing in this type of setting then he was truly, and completely, barking mad.

The Battery

Following the path along, one comes to The Battery – a small crenellated platform jutting out on to the river. The Battery dates from the end of the 1700s and may have been part of the river defences against Napoleon. Two cannon still lie pointing out over the water. There are good views upstream to the village of Dittisham; across the river to the Anchor Stone and downstream to Noss Creek. The Anchor Stone, or 'Scold Stone' as it is sometimes called, is surmounted by a red metal warning post, placed there to indicate the treacherous rocks after a vessel named the *William*, owned by a Mr Hall of Galmpton came to grief here in the nineteenth century. Tradition in the area has it that the unfaithful wives of the village of Ditsum (local pronunciation) were tied to the stone as a 'punishment for their sins'.

Agatha Christie enthusiasts will delight in sitting on the battlements next to one of the cannon and recreating a well-known picture taken at this very spot of herself and her husband. It was also here in the novel *Five Little Pigs*, that the body of Amyas (a character named after her childhood sweetheart, mentioned in the chapter on Anstey's Cove) is found dead amongst his paints and canvases, poisoned, albeit painlessly, by coniine (spotted hemlock).

The Anchor Stone

The Battery

The Camellia Garden

(Right) The heronry

A red camellia

(Right) Fireburst

Before you leave, take a close look at the river banks. Herons are commonplace (there is a heronry in the trees further down the river), but score extra I-spy points for seals, egrets and, if you are very, very fortunate, those minute flashes of orange and ultramarine – kingfishers.

The path now rises more steeply to the Camellia Garden. The walls were built by Spanish prisoners of war in Sir Humphrey Gilbert's era. There is a solitary cork oak (another clue in the murder fête) and camellias everywhere. To see them at their best, visit in February or March. Agatha Christie, apparently, had a preference for this season. As well as the camellias, bright red and white rhododendrons burst up through the bare tangle of deciduous trees like so many enormous firework displays. I am inspired to write my own invernal Wabi Sabian haki:

Grey, leafless branches.
Red upward fireburst of bloom.
Winter. In Death, Life.

The path continues upwards, past a mysterious abandoned and rusty safe lying in the shrubbery, towards the house.

Pink magnolia behind the house

* * * * * *

The library, Greenway

I was lucky enough to get a place on the final tour around Greenway House before the much-needed restoration work began. As a Christie fan, entering this inner sanctum provoked a feeling of butterflies. Many rooms had hardly changed since Agatha Christie's residence. Odd things stick in your mind – a pile of hats one on top of each other in the entrance hall; a huge bundle of clearly tried-and-tested walking sticks; an umbrella stand full of golf clubs.

The front room looking out over the gardens was decorated solely with china and furniture (surprisingly delicate and slender) from her childhood home, Ashfield. There was a wonderful painting of the novelist as a child.

The library, apart from her books, revealed the blue and white frieze painted during the war by one of the officers of the US Patrol Boat flotilla stationed here and which traces their exploits through the conflict. The nude was apparently a local 'beauty'.

The drawing room housed Agatha's grand piano – she had reached concert standard and was only prevented from making a career of it by her overwhelming performance nerves (one wonders about our SATS-driven education when we see the results achieved by Christie who received no formal schooling to speak of). There were two armchairs either side of the fireplace, one for Max and one for herself where she used to sit every Christmas and read her latest work to the family. Max, famously, would invariably nod off during the proceedings only to awake at the last moment and again, invariably, announce the correct name of the murderer, something which infuriated her.

Upstairs, we saw the huge, silver and mother-of-pearl chest of drawers mentioned at length in her autobiography, once home to the champing worm; also her travelling bed from the archaeological digs in Iraq. And everywhere – on book-shelves, sideboards, tables and dressing tables – objects picked up (they were avid collectors) by herself and her husband during their travels around the world.

In Max's bedroom, our guide explained that due to the settling of the building's foundations and subsequent ingress of water, the entire wall of the room had been in imminent danger of falling away from the rest of the house. Stories have it that the whole structure been held in place by a bookcase which stretched the length of the room. If true, it seems fitting that books, at the end of the day, had saved this part of the magnificent house from collapse.

At the reopening of the house in the Spring of 2009 there was talk of being able to rent rooms upstairs for the weekend and take dinner, in full evening dress of course, in her dining room with a butler and all. Who knows, maybe one day I'll get that set before cocktails…

But that is for the future. For the moment we have more than enough with the garden: Max's giant, contorted pink magnolia next to the tennis court, thickets of black bamboo and enormous tree ferns, *Pieris japonica* as tall as houses, and blood-red camellias. The boathouse, The Battery, the river. Greenway is a very special place that draws one to revisit time and time again.

2
ASHFIELD

Home

You can visit all the towns, beaches and gardens, churches, hotels, and houses mentioned in this book, except for one: Ashfield – the house where Agatha Christie was born.

Walking back to my car, after a talk at Torquay Museum by Agatha's grandson, Mathew Prichard, a question keeps running through my mind. How did Ashfield, the home of the most famous detective novelist the world has ever seen, which fans from all over the world would have flocked to see, manage to get itself demolished?

The Herald Express, 1 October 1960, reported that an application had been made by Capital Development Co Ltd to bulldoze 2 Victorian villas: Heathcourt no.21, and Ashfield no.15, Barton Road, Torquay. The plan is to build two six-storey blocks, totalling 64 flats, and a petrol station in their place. The proposal is turned down (objections to the filling station), but the principle of flats is agreed.

Is it possible that nobody knew who had grown up in that house? Agatha tells us herself that when she heard from a friend of the designs on Ashfield, she rushed to her solicitor and asked if she could buy the property back – make a gift of it, perhaps, as an old people's home.

The reply was that the process could not be stopped. And, having shunned publicity all her life, Agatha Christie was certainly not going to kick up a fuss about it.

The facts alone, however, should have spoken, more than eloquently, on her behalf. The 'Queen of Crime', had already published over 80 works and sold millions of books all over the world. 'The Mousetrap' had taken its place in the *Guinness Book of Records* back on 12 April 1958 when it became the longest

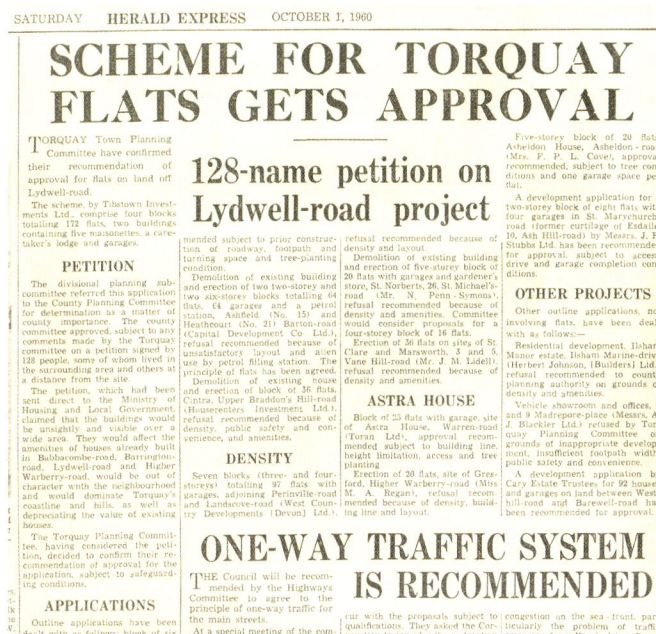

The demolition of Ashfield, featured in the Herald Express

running West End show of all time – 2239 performances. By the beginning of the sixties, the 5000 mark was in sight.

But, incredibly, in perhaps the most colossal lack of foresight ever perpetrated by a local council, Torquay town planners allow the development to proceed.

A year or so later, Agatha Christie commits the one error she has told us all through her autobiography to avoid – she goes back to Barton Road – to the scene of the crime – to look for a memory.

She is devastated. There is nothing left; everything has been obliterated. The sole survivor is a monkey puzzle tree, forgotten, neglected and dying in a back yard.

She realizes Ashfield and everything that went with it is over. Only a ghost of a little girl playing with a hoop will linger in this place where she had once been so happy.

She says a poignant goodbye and with that brings the autobiography, her life-story, to a close.

* * * * * *

Torquay 1880. While her husband is away on business in America, the newly-married Clara Miller has been instructed to look for a villa to rent. She visits 35 different properties but is unimpressed. Then she sees Ashfield, falls in love with it and since it is only for sale and not for rent, she buys it on impulse with £2000 that she has inherited from an uncle.

Agatha Christie is playfully dismissive of the house; it wasn't anything out of the ordinary and not even in the fashionable parts of Torquay, that is, the Lincombes (overlooking Meadfoot) or the Warberries (overlooking everything). But it was by no means a modest or small house. Built on two and three storeys as the Victorian loved, it came with a conservatory full of palms and aspidistras, and a 'mature' garden with a variety of trees.

The house was almost on the crest of the rocky hill above Tor and had wonderful sea views. Behind was virtually open country. Fields and woods swept on and down towards Shiphay Lane. They were surrounded by other large villas: above on the corner was Heathcourt; below them St Mary's, Oakhill, Florian, Eltham and the extensive grounds of The Elms. All have since gone.[1]

Ashfield is where Agatha Christie was born, where her daughter Rosalind was born, and where her mother and father lived out their lives. It was the setting for a very happy childhood and she begged her mother to keep it on after the death of her father.

There is a room in Greenway which she decorated and furnished as if it was Ashfield with many of her father's often extravagant, sometimes unwise acquisitions: paintings, china, furniture and ornaments.

Ashfield was the place that, as she grew older, she returned to in her dreams. Not Greenway nor Wallingford – but Ashfield. Agatha even suggests Max was slightly jealous of the place because he had never been part of it. Did he subconsciously push for its sale and for the purchase of Greenway in 1938 out of this insecurity?

The family 'only' had the three or four servants (which apparently was then a minimum!) – having to forgo the luxury of a butler or coach- and footmen. The 1901 census shows seven people living at the house – Frederick 54, Clarissa, 46, and children Margaret and Agatha, 22 and 10 respectively, all living by 'their own means'. Then there was Jane Rowe, 49, the cook from Jacobstowe; Marie Sige (from France), 22, the lady's maid; Elizabeth Williams, a parlourmaid from Helston in Cornwall, and finally Louisa Barter, the housemaid from Brixham. All of these names are wonderfully brought to life in the first part of Agatha's autobiography.

Jane was certainly good at her job, and the menus were sumptuous, at least up to the time Agatha's father died, when the purse strings had to be tightened somewhat.

They had some illustrious literary guests; Henry James and Rudyard Kipling, for example, came to visit. This was probably thanks to the family's connections with the very popular local writer of the time, Eden Phillpotts, himself a friend of Thomas Hardy and much loved for his series of Dartmoor novels. He lived only a stone's throw away across Oakhill Road at Eltham.

Most of all, the young Agatha loved the garden; she knew the names of all the trees and shrubs: the ilex, the cedar, the towering Wellingtonia and the araucaria – the monkey puzzle tree. The trees would become her friends and companions during the years she spent here alone (she never really went to school) with her widowed mother, after her sister Madge married and moved away. And, as at Greenway, the garden also had a corner for a dog's cemetery, complete with headstones.

Ashfield was clearly the custodian of many of the keys to unlock the character of Agatha Christie.

But where was Ashfield exactly? Walking up Barton Road, the blue plaque of the Torbay Civic Society gives a rough indication. Agatha Christie, herself, says that when she returned to

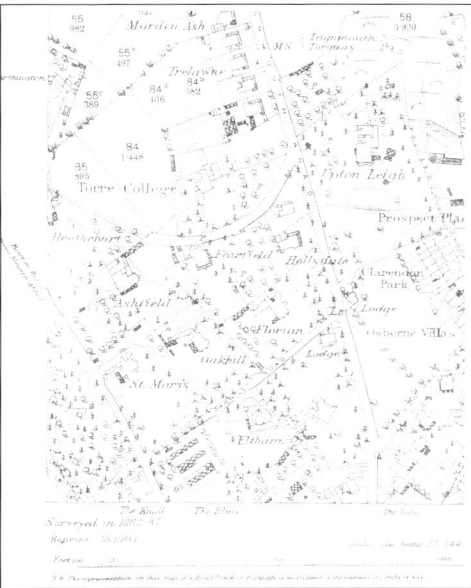

(Left) Ashfield plaque

(Right) Map of Ashfield c.1860

(Left) Flats on the former site of the tennis court of Heathcourt

(Right) The scraggy yew tree

View from Barton Road over Torbay

the site in the early sixties she could not work out where the house had stood. Ordnance Survey maps of the time, and the account of her childhood, give us some clues to work with. Surely we owe it to the creator of Hercule Poirot to undertake a little detection and identify the precise location.

One of the difficult things to comprehend is the size of the plot. It covered roughly two acres. Today, there are 12 reasonably-sized houses, gardens and a road on the grounds of Ashfield.

If we stand in front of the plaque, then the block of flats on the left stands on what would have been the tennis court of the adjacent property, Heathcourt.

To your right, just at the end of the parking bay is a scraggy yew tree. You can see here what is left of the corner wall of the property that once comprised Ashfield. Near this point was the main entrance with its drive curving up to the house.

Walking down Barton Road towards the town, the west boundary wall (much reduced) runs down to your left along the front of the houses. You start to see the views that Agatha Christie complained were lost when the Boys' Grammar School was built in the 1920s. Over to the right is Berry Head and then Elbury and Broadsands come into sight. You would also have been able to see Waldon Hill straight ahead.

Just before the entrance to Kiddy Import and Export you can see the large lower corner walls with their buttresses. Eden Phillpotts' house was down the next left – Oakhill Road. Good on plaques, but not so hot on conservation, the council has placed another blue circle there for us to admire.

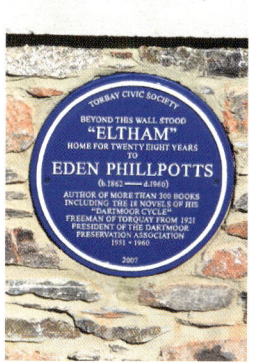

(Left) Plaque marking Eden Phillpotts' house

(Right) The bottom wall of the garden

The bottom corner of the garden

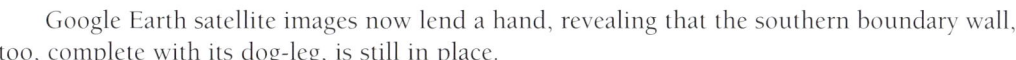

Google Earth satellite images now lend a hand, revealing that the southern boundary wall, too, complete with its dog-leg, is still in place.

To see where the house itself would have stood, we need to walk back up Barton Road and then turn right into St Vincent's Road. In her autobiography Agatha talks of a kitchen garden, bounded by a high wall which abutted the road. And there it is, opposite Mt Stuart Hospital. The strange dead-end you can see was the back entrance to Ashfield, which once led through potting sheds to the back of the house.

As we walk into St Vincent's Close we can see that the back gardens of the present houses are on a higher level – these are the remains of the raised kitchen garden. If we stand in front of no.3 then the house would have covered all the land from this house, across the road as far as the houses opposite.

The front door of Ashfield looked down towards Barton Road. As you walked up the slope from the main gate, the famous monkey puzzle would have stood to your right. A vine-bearing trellis covered the façade. The porch itself was covered in ivy or creepers. The room on the left-hand corner was the dining room. The tennis court looked down on the house through the trees.

There is an amusing passage in the autobiography when a friend of the family, Lord Lifford, calls when the family is out. The maid doesn't recognise him, refuses to let him in and runs up to the first floor lavatory window to tell him to leave. He convinces her that he is genuine by showing his

Ashfield's rear entrance

knowledge of the house and telling her which room she is bawling from. Embarrassed, she lets him in. This window must be the small one above the porch to the left.

There is a photo of the entrance hall in the exhibition housed at Torquay Museum. Agatha says that the lavatory was in a most unfortunate position being clearly visible from the hall at the top of the stairs. If you were caught in there when guests arrived you had no alternative but to sit it out until they had gone before making your exit. So it is in the photo; the stairs were to the left and doubled back on themselves to the first floor. The floor is tiled and decorated with a pair of rugs. In the far corner is a fireplace, its mantelpiece laden with ornaments. A huge grandfather clock stands at the foot of the stairs.

Outside once again, the right-hand corner of the front elevation was the famous Kai-Kai greenhouse, described in such detail in *Postern of Fate* and which contained Mathilde, the rocking horse, and the buggy of American origin called Truelove. Agatha would have driven this buggy down the slope, which ran from the kitchen garden in front of the conservatory and Kai-Kai, down to the monkey puzzle tree.

The conservatory occupied the right half of the south façade and was fronted by potted plants and statues. Above it was the tower, an extra storey built by Agatha's father to provide additional bedrooms. Rosalind's bedroom would later be here, and George Pepper, the son of the family's housekeeper would describe how he and Rosalind would climb up the trellis to her room.

As I have hinted, many of the details outlined above and many more besides were destined to make one final appearance…

Postern of Fate was the last of the novels published in her lifetime. At first sight, it is a strange, oddly rambling novel. That's because, more than a detective story, it is a book of distant reminiscences, about Ashfield

It is, as Max Mallowan says, a book for the initiated, full of private memories and jokes that only those nearest to her would recognize. Things like her comments on the use of 'you know' by youngsters nowadays. The fact that Tuppence eats all the pips in her grapes. The reference to Corbyn Head. So many quirky little episodes, so many seemingly irrelevant facts about the contents and layout of the house.

But not irrelevant for her. She is aware that this will probably be her last book, and is determined to set it all down. She is going to make one last journey back to her beloved Ashfield and this time she doesn't care what anyone thinks.

One of the characters even comments 'Who'd read a book like that?' and she says with a tongue-in-cheek smile, because she is Agatha Christie and she knows it is true: 'You'd be surprised what people will read – and enjoy.'

NOTES

[1] The right-hand side of Barton Road has fared better as regards the developers. The Knoll, if you peer over the wall towards the bottom, is still there, although it's slowly sinking under the surrounding development. During Agatha's adolescence, Ernest Shackleton's brother lived here and the explorer spent three months at the Knoll in 1907 before leaving Torbay on the *Nimrod* as Commander of the British Antartic Expedition.

3
ALL SAINTS

A Christening

All Saints Church is built at the intersection of the two oldest thoroughfares in Torquay. For centuries, the original Torquay to Paignton road crossed Walden Hill, descended today's Croft road, passed the local mill here at Mill Lane, skirted the recreation ground and then continued on to Livermead. The other road ran south-north away from the seafront, along

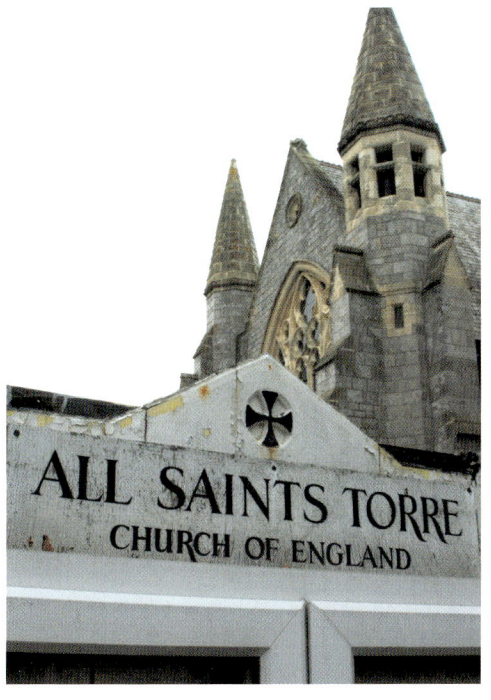

(Left) All Saints Church, Torre

(Right) Sunlight on the West Front

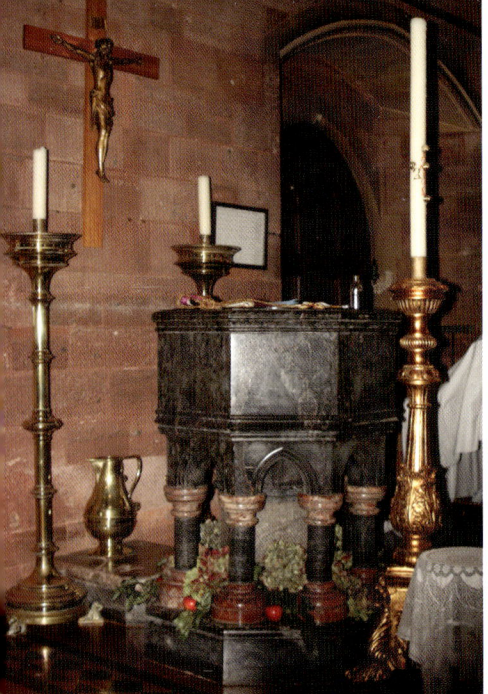

The font where Agatha Miller was baptized at All Saints Church

present-day Belgrave Road and then up along Barton Road following the high ground towards Newton Abbot.

The Millers lived in Barton Road just a few hundreds yards away from All Saints. When the original church of Tormohun could no longer cope with the ever increasing number of parishioners, Frederick Miller was one of the major financial contributors to the building of the new church. He made Agatha one of the founders and this is where she was baptized.

It's Sunday and so, hopefully, I'll find it open today. The morning service has just finished – three Men of the Cloth are climbing into a waiting car to make their getaway… and yet the doors are already being locked. The man with the keys, a very dapper gentleman in a Prince of Wales check, offers, very kindly, to reopen and let me look around for a few minutes. Once in, he rushes off to silence the bleeping. I comment that these are sad times we live in when even churches have not only to be locked but alarmed into the bargain. He agrees: 'We have to, or they'd pinch everything!'

The elegant, black-veined-with-pink, marble font lies just to the left of the door and, behind it on the wall, there is an extract from the register of baptisms. It records that on 20 November 1890, the Reverend Majendie officiating, Agatha Mary Clarissa Miller was christened. She was named Mary after her grandmother; Clarissa was, of course, her mother's name; and Agatha, apparently, was hit upon by a friend as they walked down to the service. We shall see who this was later.

Her father Frederick's occupation is given as 'Gentleman'. In the 1891 census, he is recorded as having 'no occupation'; in 1901, he is living 'on own means'. Agatha Christie, too, saw no particular merit in having a job if one didn't need the money and extolled the virtues of having time, and thus the possibility of choosing and planning one's days exactly as one wants.

And so, Frederick Alvah Miller, the wealthy American from New York, lived a life of leisure. He used to spend his mornings at the Royal Torbay Yacht Club playing cards and conversing. He would go back to Ashfield for lunch and later return to spend the afternoons once again at the club. Then he would take a cab home and dress for dinner. It was a very pleasant, civilized and privileged existence.

Extract from the registry of baptisms at All Saints.

He had, by all accounts, a great sense of humour. He was immensely popular with his peers, and as an American resident in Torquay at that time he would have been quite an exotic bird. On top of this, it was also rumoured that he had had a fling with the Brooklyn beauty, Jenny Jerome, who would later become Lady Randolph Churchill. He was said to bear more than a passing resemblance to the Prince of Wales, what with his hat, beard and rather portly stature. But on looking at a photo of the future Edward VII and his cronies on a visit to Torquay around this time, it would seem that every man in the country was a Bertie look-alike.

The Cricket Ground with the oak tree

Every Sunday, in the cricket season, Frederick spent his time at the Torquay Cricket Club – often taking the young Agatha along to help score the matches under the great oak tree (which is still there), next to the pavilion in Cricketfield Road.

What, I hear you asking incredulously, an American not only interested in, but even understanding, the game of cricket? The baptism register solves this puzzle. There, in the last column set aside for the signatures of the sponsors, is the answer: W. H. Kitson.

Kitson was a big name in Victorian Torquay. William Henry's father, William Kitson, is widely credited with having virtually transformed single-handedly the rough and ready Tor Quay into the undisputed Queen of the English Riviera. A solicitor working for the Palk family, the landowners of the Warberries and the Lincombes, it was he who carved out the concentric circles of roads around the hills, and laid out and sold the plots for the luxurious villas and gardens which would come to characterize the town in the mid to late 1800s.

William Kitson also founded Torquay Cricket Club, and his son, W. H. Kitson was responsible later for the erection of the pavilion. William Henry was friend, neighbour and cricket mentor to the Millers. He lived two villas up from Ashfield at Hemsworth, which stood on the site of the present day primary school.

The Millers were well connected. They knew the Kitsons, the Palks, the Carys of Torre Abbey, the Mallocks who owned Cockington, and also had links with the local artistic community through their friendship with another neighbour, the writer, Eden Phillpotts. Agatha's mother was a great admirer of his garden with its exotic plants, tulip trees and ponds.

Frederick Miller worked tirelessly for his beloved cricket club. He endeavoured to alleviate its financial difficulties by organizing amateur dramatic productions to raise money at the Abbey Theatre and the Bath Saloon. It is clear where Agatha's love of the theatre stemmed from.

Sadly, in 1900, it fell to him, as Vice President, to announce the winding up of the club; there simply was not enough support, enthusiasm or money to carry on. In March 1901, therefore, the club did not renew the lease at Cricketfield Road and officially ceased to exist. The following November, Frederick Miller died.

The memories of her father were incredibly precious for Agatha. She confessed years later in an interview, that when driving down to Greenway from London she always got her chauffeur to make a detour so she could see the oak tree at the cricket field where they used to sit together on sunny, summer afternoons.

The other two witnesses at the baptism are interesting, too. The first is the grand-sounding Capt. The Hon. A.R. Hewitt RN. This is Viscount Lifford, of Irish descent, the same Lord Lifford mentioned in the 'lavatory window' episode in the autobiography and described in an earlier chapter. Agatha regularly visited Ireland at the beginning of the 1900s.

The last name is that of James Sullivan. He is the husband of beloved Aunt Cassie, an American living in New York with whom Agatha spent time at the end of her world tour with her first husband, Archie. Agatha tells us that she was one of her mother's best friends. Surely Cassie is the one who on the way to the church came up with the name Agatha?

I am aware that my guide to All Saints, a former churchwarden, is probably anxious to get back for his sirloin and Yorkshires and so it's just one more quick question before I leave. Where did Agatha and her father sit?

All Saints Church, seen as you arrive from Barton Road

The pew used by Agatha and her father at All Saints

There is the pew, fifth back on the left (Agatha had said in the autobiography that it was 'near the front'). 'We've been meaning to get a plaque for it – but just haven't got round to it yet.' my guide explains apologetically.

Before I leave, he tells me 'It is a pity Hilary isn't here – she could tell you some stories – she used to be friends with the gardener up at Ashfield.'

I make a modest contribution to the church fund and receive a promise that he'll pass on Hilary's number to me.

I give Hilary a ring. She seems a bit confused by the gardener connection – but she does know loads about Agatha Christie and she would be most willing to talk to me. She used to attend the Girls' Grammar School and her French teacher, Miss Petty, was the daughter of the vicar that succeeded the Reverend Majendie. She recalled that Agatha would often call the Reverend Petty when she needed some advice about technical church matters for her books. Agatha wrote a dedication in his copy of *Three Act Tragedy* thanking him for his ecclesiastical advice. She would visit the vicarage with her mother, for tea and cucumber sandwiches, served on a magnificent Indian tray with a samovar as a centerpiece. Agatha would always arrive with her mother in a long black dress and a picture hat and you could hear the tap-tap-tap of Mrs Miller's silver-headed ebony cane long before they arrived.

Clarissa Miller was a tall, austere, almost severe looking woman. She was definitely the more introverted of the couple. The autobiography tells that often she would see her husband gazing out of the window and ask, 'What are you thinking about?' to which her husband would answer 'Nothing'. Christie says that this was most probably true but that Clarissa found this ability of her spouse to completely suspend his mental processes something totally incomprehensible. Christie gives her almost clairvoyant powers, claiming she knew what family members were thinking before they even opened their mouths.

My lunch-hour is up – I promise to pop back later to All Saints to see the Christmas Tree Fair, one of the highlights of the church year. Different charities decorate in their own individual styles up to fifty fir trees which then stand as a guard of honour around the church. It's a wonderful sight. All Saints Church continues to be actively involved with, and still plays a vibrant and vital role in, the local community. Frederick Alvah must be up there somewhere, in the Yacht Club in the sky, stroking his beard with pride.

The All Saints Church banner

The Christmas Tree Festival

4
THE PRINCESS PIER

Rollerskating

The Princess Pier was named after the fourth of Queen Victoria's daughters, Louise Caroline Alberta, who was later, as the wife of the Governor of Canada, to give her name to the Canadian Province of Alberta.

Princess Pier

Marvellous original ironwork

She was a talented woman – an accomplished writer, sculptor and artist. She had first visited the town at the end of 1887. She and her husband, the Marquis of Lorne, arrived in the town incognito, booking into the Western Hotel (later to become the Grand) as Mr and Mrs Campbell. Two days later they moved to Cumper's Hotel (which became the Torbay Hotel) as she required a more sheltered position.

This strange episode is perhaps explained by the fact that there seems to have been an official and unofficial side to the Marquis of Lorne. Officially, in 1878, Benjamin Disraeli had used his powers of persuasion to get Queen Victoria to appoint the Marquis of Lorne, her son-in-law, as Governor of Canada. She eventually agreed, appreciating the immense honour involved, but was heart-broken at the thought of being separated from her beloved daughter.

The unofficial version is that Lord Lorne was a rampant homosexual, prone to meeting guardsmen in Hyde Park, until his exile to the land of the larch, the pine, Mounties and wild flowers.

Had they been rumbled at the Western Hotel, was it really the weather, or did the Marquis just prefer the proximity to Princess Gardens?

Enough Victorian gossip. The couple came back openly in 1890 and the Princess laid the foundation stone for the pier. The Rev. Majendie was on hand to preside and a member of the Kitson family signed the memorial stone which now stands outside the Princess Theatre.

(Left) A postcard of 1910 showing the pavilion on the pier

(Right) Concerts on the pier, 1931

Relaxing on the pier

We can see from postcards that in Agatha's time there was a pavilion at the end of the pier and a bowling green at the landward end on the site of the present-day, glass-walled café. Rollerskating was in vogue. There was a choice for skaters between the Assembly rooms of the Marine Spa at Beacon Cove – decidedly high class – or the pier which Agatha and her friends, despite the rough surface, preferred. It cost twopence a session. Her skating partners were the Lucy sisters, and it was their brother, Reggie Lucy, to whom Agatha would eventually become engaged.

The pier was also the point of embarkation for a boat trip mentioned in the autobiography that Agatha made with her brother, Monty. Her mother thought she was sensible enough not to fall overboard and was happy that Monty was taking time out with his little sister. Her mother had second thoughts as she handed the girl down to her brother in the waiting dinghy, remembering as they sped off across the choppy water her own delicate seafaring stomach. Agatha was to find out unfortunately (three times on this voyage) that she had inherited this particular maternal trait.

    I must say I, personally, only really discovered the pier while writing this book, having passed by thousands of times but never ventured out along its length. It is popular with anglers – mackerel, gold and grey mullet, wrasse and bass are all up for grabs. The local fisherman's website recommends the 'mark' but warns of the large numbers of 'numpteys' in the high season. For those who are interested, every day in the summer, a page in the *Herald Express*, is devoted to the previous day's sport around the bay. Articles assiduously report species, weight, and bait used, accompanied by the obligatory picture of proud angler holding catch aloft.

    What the pier does offer is another perspective of the town. It's a reminder of how, just by changing your viewpoint only slightly, things can be seen in a totally different light.

An opportunity for an Agatha Christie cruise

Evening draws in

An afternoon stroll

5
BEACON COVE

An early start at Torquay Yacht Club

Bathing – ladies only

I park the car and look down on a sea of multi-coloured sails assembled on the quay. Torquay Yacht Club is clearly still thriving and up very early on this Sunday morning, too.

I've come to look for The Ladies' Bathing Cove.

Bathing was governed (for certain classes) by strict rules when Agatha was a young woman. For many years, there was segregation between the sexes. The main bathing beach for women was at Beacon Cove (then known simply as the Ladies Bathing Cove). Meadfoot was a 'progressive' mixed-bathing beach, an activity still frowned upon by many councillors. And yet despite this prudery, just along the road at Abbey Sands, a visitor staying at the Imperial Hotel notes in her diary: 'As we passed along the road at this part, a number of working men (it was Saturday afternoon) whisked off their clothes at the wall on the beach and ran like savages to the water, which is not well adapted for bathing.'[1]

Hypocrisy was rife too. In her autobiography Agatha Christie points out that the cove was hidden from view, and no male was allowed within 50 yards of the beach. Yet the raft which she used to swim out to was visible from Torbay Royal Yacht Club. Curiously enough, the club had had to move from their original site, at the bottom of the Terrace, to this perfect vantage point in 1886. Members would spice up their reading of the morning papers by spying on the assembled beauties with opera glasses. As it is Agatha who recounts this, the ladies, presumably, were also conscious of what was going on.[2]

Christie describes in a wonderful passage the rigamarole of the bathing machine. The price was sixpence for the first half hour and then sixpence for each additional quarter hour. For this sum the bathing machine owner was duty bound to provide customers with two towels and a bathing costume. Once inside you were jolted and shaken as the machine was let down towards the water. Then you changed into the latest fashion – the alpaca swimsuit. How much this must have itched and how heavy it must have been when wet! More worryingly, who had been wearing it before you?

Beacon Cove

AGATHA CHRISTIE'S DEVON

Living Coasts

Maybe the cumbersome weight of this bathing attire had something to do with the incident she recounts where the young Agatha almost drowned while swimming out to the raft with her nephew, Jack, on her back. She was only saved, in extremis, by the prompt intervention of the bathing attendant.

Making my way to see the Ladies Bathing Cove I realised I hadn't noticed, or heard about it, for many years. Where had it gone, how did I get there? I knew more or less where to look and, on discovering it, realised why it had passed me by for so long.

The entrance is all but hidden. A narrow alley between boarding that could easily be the entrance to a building site. A small, mean, brass plaque reminds the reader why the old swimming baths and assembly rooms (the Marine Spa) had been closed down. A tragic accident, resulting in the death of a young swimmer in July 1971, harrowed all of us youngsters who had just days before been swimming in the same pool.

The entrance to the Cove is obscured due to the siting here of Living Coasts, an annexe of Paignton Zoo. A massive construction of netting and steel poles houses seabirds whose fellows wheel around free in the skies only metres away. The net is surrounded by metres and metres of security fencing – it looks more like a concentration camp than an aviary.

BEACON COVE

Shag drying its wings

A view across the Cove.

Old photos confirm my own memories that the Cove used to be amazingly popular, with hardly a square metre of beach left to sit on. Here, as at other points in the bay, an attraction has been created at the expense of the very natural beauty that brought people here in the first place.

The Cove in the early morning is silent perfection. A shag, on a triangular rock off-shore, extends and flaps its wings to dry them in the rising sun. The light is streaming over the cliffs, and a fine mist is suspended above the calm sea.

Sitting on the step, it's just me, the cormorant and a man fishing from his boat. The Cove could easily have remained the focal point of this part of the coast. Amenities and attractions could have been built around it to enhance the inherent loveliness of the spot. As it is, the aviary has been arbitrarily imposed on a Cove treasured by Agatha Christie in her youth, ringed with barbed wire. Puffins, guillemots and kittiwakes are caged in. So is this fine beach.

The Imperial Hotel beach at dawn

NOTES

[1] We will have occasion to note elsewhere the Janus-like face of Victorian society, where contradiction and paradox could exist side by side. It was the same when it came to nudity and sexuality. Prostitution and associated diseases were rife among the lower classes and yet in the higher echelons of society the untimely showing of an ankle could be a social gaffe.

[2] The whole of this section of the autobiography – the first flirtations and descriptions of proposals – conveys beautifully the latent, repressed desire of the times and what it must have been like having to restrain such basic instincts.

6
MEADFOOT BEACH

Bathing – mixed

I turn up Ilsham Marine Drive. It's about 8.30am and parents are dropping off their children at the neighbourhood's exclusive private school. It seems that every other car has a personalised number plate. Marine Drive, as you will see, is to Torquay what the community of Bel Air is to Los Angeles.

At the top of the rise there are magnificent views on a clear, crisp morning like today across to Teignmouth and, beyond, to Lyme Regis in Dorset. The road curves and the promontory of Hope's Nose is spread below you, the sea sparkling in the sunshine. It descends, and what I

View across to Teignmouth

Looking out over Hope's Nose

think is the best view of Torbay, unfurls. The barren cliffs of Thatcher Rock lie just off-shore, a posse of Brixham trawlers clustered around. In the background lies Berry Head and then the whole magnificent sweep of Torbay.

This stunning panorama is the main reason why the properties that overlook this view command the prices they do, often in the millions. One, a gleaming white modern design of steel and glass, is a far cry from the elegant homes that Agatha Christie would have seen being erected here, but it has the most amazing outlook over the grassy slopes that run down to the cliffs, out over Thatcher Rock and the sweep of the bay.

A plaque reveals that these seven or so acres of grass and Scots pines tumbling towards the sea were generously donated to Torbay Council as parkland by an anonymous (obviously anti-developmental) benefactor in the sixties. Apparently, cattle are left to graze here for three or four months of the year to keep the vegetation under control, though I have never seen them. Further down the slope, a small grass and stone amphitheatre has been created where Shakespeare plays are performed on summer evenings.

The road winds down towards Meadfoot beach. The terrain is a dry, craggy, ochre. The overarching trees have silvery leaves, not unlike olives. The sun, streaming through, dapples the road; the sea beyond is deepest blue, and you could easily imagine yourself somewhere in Liguria or on the French Riviera.

Thatcher Rock with the theatre to the right

AGATHA CHRISTIE'S DEVON

A scene on the Italian Riviera?

(Below left) Kilmorie today

(Right) An old postcard with Kilmorie visible in the background

To your right, the enormous retaining walls of a lost garden march up the hill. A hillock with balustrade and cannon is visible up through the trees. Shortly, a pleasant drive of well-tended exotic plants leads off to an enormous block of flats. The name, Kilmorie, is the same as the villa they replaced. Marine Drive wasn't opened until 1924 but the young Agatha Christie would have certainly known and probably visited Kilmorie and its gardens. Sir Thomas Bazely, a retired Manchester cotton magnate, had created here a vast, wonderland of rhododendrons, azaleas, veronicas and other imported species – maybe an influence for the future Greenway. The *Torquay Directory* of May 1911 gives the following description of the vista from his

MEADFOOT BEACH

Meadfoot looking towards Hope's Nose

Looking towards Daddyhole Plain

The bathing beach today

The bathing beach in the early 1900s

astronomical observatory: 'the view of the bay is uninterrupted and magnificent with Berry Head and the English Channel beyond. The prospect is said to resemble the Bay of Naples, omitting Vesuvius!'

The thickly wooded frontage of the beach has, unlike Cliff Walk above the Princess Gardens, remained undeveloped. There are, however, for those who wish to find them, marvellous woodland paths high above the road, hidden from view, where you can walk listening to the sound of the waves below.

Swimming was one of Agatha Christie's great passions in life. It is always first on the list of favourite things that she does, or, later, of things that she misses because she can no longer indulge them. Taking a tram to the Strand and then walking, or even walking all the way – almost 2 miles – from Ashfield, she would brave wind and rain to go swimming with her sister, Madge, when the latter was down for the summer with her son, Jack.

The road the three would have walked up from the Strand to get to the beach, Meadfoot Road, still has most of its Italianate villas intact. Many have been turned into hotels, offices, rest homes or flats, and more than one is looking a little the worst for wear, but, walking up the hill you are seeing more or less what Agatha, Madge and Jack would have seen a century ago. A fountain at the top of the hill, set in a corner wall, bears the date 1859. Jack would have probably stopped here for a cool mouthful after his exertions and his habit of naming every villa they passed, together with name of the owner.

Agatha Christie preferred Meadfoot to Beacon Cove as it was bigger and wider. She must have really been a strong swimmer because the 'accessible' rock she talks of in the middle of the bay is an awfully long way out. Being of independent spirit, she might also have preferred it

Hesketh Crescent

(Left) View from The Osborne over Thatcher Rock

(Right) From The Osborne towards Berry Head

because it was the only mixed bathing beach. She does note though that men were often too embarrassed to turn up and risk seeing their female acquaintances in what was still, for many, considered a shocking state of semi-nudity.

Bathing was at the end of the beach where today the beach-huts are sited. At that time, however, there were no concrete tiers. The cliffs finished on the sand and there was a flight of steps leading down. People remained fully dressed if not bathing, often with parasols. Then, of course, there were the ubiquitous bathing machines.

Overlooking the beach stands the magnificent buff-coloured sweep of Hesketh Crescent. Designed by the brothers William and John Harvey, and completed in 1848, it has to be the most spectacularly located Regency crescent in England. Famous residents have included Charles Darwin on a short-stay at No.2, working on the third edition of *On the Origin of Species*, and the novelist Henry James. Angela Burdett-Coutts, one of the richest, most powerful, philanthropic and learned women of the Victorian era, lived here at No.1.

In *Sleeping Murder*, the location for the crime, Dillmouth, has many similarities with Torquay (the scene change to Torquay at the end of the novel is pure playfulness on the part of the author). Agatha Christie might have had The Osborne in mind when she wrote of The Royal Clarence Hotel. (She does, however, describe the Clarence as bow-fronted not crescent-shaped so maybe the Torbay Hotel is also a contender.)

Before returning home, I pop in to see a friend who lives nearby. He is fortunate enough to own a villa which is virtually intact as regards décor, fixtures and fittings from the end of the Victorian era. As something of an antique collector, he has also decked out the house in period furniture. It's like stepping back in time some hundred years. Sitting on the veranda in the sun, glass of wine in hand, contemplating the view out over Meadfoot towards Thatcher Rock, it's easy to understand why back then, all over Europe, Torquay was known as the Queen of Watering Places.

7
COCKINGTON

The water meadow path

The Stage

Turn off the main road from Torquay to Paignton and in less than a minute you are in the middle of the countryside. It's an example of *rus in urbe* to make Nero proud. The footpath leads through a wood-lined water meadow. A wooden causeway snakes up the valley, crossing and recrossing, amongst reeds and wild daffodils, the ice-clear stream.

You enter Cockington park through a gatehouse built by the Mallock family in the 1920s; a last-ditch attempt to keep the public out of their woodland sanctuary. The path rises up through a series of muddy ponds (supposedly built by the monks of Torre Abbey to keep them in fresh fish), today policed by mallard and moorhen. Occasionally, a gigantic carp glides through the murk.

The landscape is primeval. Plants here grow huge. Gunnera, enormous spiky rhubarb, towers above you with leaves 2 metres across. There are giant palms. Rhododendrons reach 20, 30 metres into the sky. Ferns are everywhere.

A hart's tongue and moss-lined corridor of every conceivable shade of green leads under a bridge that carries the

(Left) A female mallard

(Centre) Gunnera

(Right) A towering magnolia

Cockington Manor

Agatha, the rising star

old Paignton road on up to Occombe farm. A hollow, carpeted with yellow, orange and white daffodils and narcissi, rolls down to the path on our left. A few metres further on and the park opens up and dips and swells on to the Manor House in the distance.

Agatha would, as a young girl, have picked up her pony from the stables in Lansdowne Road, near the Conservative Club in Torre, and ridden down Mill Lane, through Chelston into Cockington.

When she grew up, she took part in amateur dramatic productions at the Mallock family home, Cockington Court. There is a photo of Agatha (in voluminous harem trousers) dressed for the rôle of Sister Anne in a humorous mélange of *Bluebeard* and *The Arabian Nights* entitled

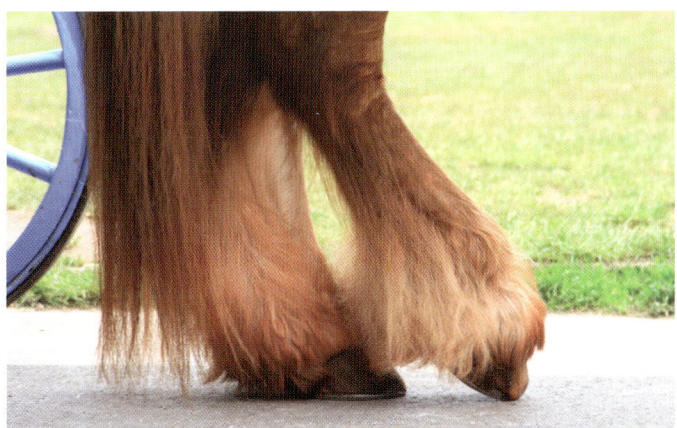

(Below left) Horse and carriage rides are still popular

(Right) A view across the park

The Bluebeard of Unhappiness. Mrs Mallock played Scheherazade. This is the Iris Mallock that she refers to as one of her best friends when she was younger.

Margaret Iris Bazeley-White married Christopher Herbert Mallock in London in 1906. The couple then returned triumphantly to Cockington as the new Lord and Lady of the Manor. CH Mallock was to die in the First World War in 1917 after inhaling mustard gas. Agatha dedicated the novel, *Why Didn't They Ask Evans?* (1924), to her son, Christopher Courtenay Mallock, adding cryptically, 'in memory of Hinds', perhaps referring to Christopher's father.

It was here then on the lawns in front of the house that Agatha Christie made her first acquaintance with the basics of theatre. I was unaware till recently that, although the novels of the 30s and 40s had brought enormous success, it was the stage productions of the early 50s, 'The Mousetrap' and 'Witness for the Prosecution', which really catapulted her to new heights of fame. On that summer evening it was, however, not the finer points of stagecraft but one of the male leads that had captured Agatha's attention – a certain Amyas (see Chapter 8).

Cockington itself, has had its own dramatic moments. Alric the Saxon, Roger de Cokynton, William de Woodland – the characters from the early days of the demesne read like the *dramatis personae* of a Blackadder episode.

Alric was the first recorded owner of Cockington. Just before the Domesday census, he sold it on to William of Falaise. William had 18 villeins, 14 serfs, 159 sheep, 42 goats and a packhorse. The whole lot was worth a tidy 50 shillings. Villeins would have some land they could cultivate for themselves. Serfs were literally slaves, owned by the Lord of the Manor. And, as their owner, he held their lives in his hand. He had the right of 'fossa and furca' – he could drown female criminals in a pit filled with water and string up male miscreants on the gallows. The gibbet was sited at Gallows Gate near Moles Hill on the present ring road. The fossa was in front of the forge. The Manor then passed to Roger de Cockington's family until the line was wiped out by the Black Death in 1348. The victims of the pestilence are buried in plague pits beneath those banks of daffodils just past the bridge we passed a moment ago.

Gallow's Gate above Cockington

The Plague Pits

Cockington, in fact, is a hybrid name meaning the settlement of the red meadow. 'Coch' was Celtic for red, the Saxon 'ing' signifies meadow and 'ton' meant village or homestead.

Fast forward three centuries and the Mallocks, goldsmiths from Exeter, buy the estate from the ill-fated Cary family in 1654.[1] Unlike their predecessors, the Mallocks were not nobility and, as members of the new upper classes, were not prepared, having made it thus far, to put up with the view of their miserable farmworkers' dwellings outside their windows.

(Left) In spring, the park at Cockington is a riot of flowers

(Right) Narcissus

For Roger Mallock, who held tenure here from 1786 for sixty years, the solution was obvious. He would simply move the village which had stood until then around the manor house – a farmyard, a dozen or so cottages, seven almshouses, a smithy and a water mill – well out of sight, down the valley.

He set about refurbishing the manor house. Then he rebuilt and prettied up the picturesque, chocolate-box cottages on their present site. He screened off his dwelling from prying eyes with trees, and landscaped the paths and approaches that we see today. He revamped the lakes and garden and built Livermead House nearby for visiting friends to use. Charles Kingsley would later feel inspired to write *The Water Babies* during a stay here.

With the arrival of the coast road and the railway, the estate became a popular destination for visitors to the Torbay. By the 1920s, the Forge, with its miniature lucky horseshoes had

The famous Cockington Forge

Looking up to the Drum Inn

become a massive tourist attraction – its image sent out on postcards all over the country. A view of the forge, the village stocks and neighbouring thatched cottages had become the brand-image for the statutory souvenir for visitors – the box of clotted cream fudge. A measure of the fame it had achieved came in 1929 when there was a rumour that the Forge was to be sold, dismantled and taken to America – lock, stocks and barrel, you might say. Irate letters to *The Times* protested that England will not be England if this destruction is continually permitted. Fortunately, the stories proved groundless.

In 1932 RH Mallock sold the estate to Cockington Trust. Ironically, while only a couple of miles away, Dartington Trust was trying to launch its modernist estate, The Cockington Trust became involved in promoting a retro-style typically English village with thatched centre. Edward Lutyens was commissioned to head the project. In the end, only the Drum Inn was built.[2]

Today Cockington is as popular as ever with walkers and holidaymakers. The Court has become a local Arts and Crafts centre, with working blacksmith, glassblower and potters. The park is still seeing performances, too. Torbay's 'Last Night of the Proms' concert is held on the lawn, in front of the manor, each summer.

NOTES

[1] After the Cockyntons, there followed a brief interlude under Walter de Woodland, an acolyte-cum-butler of the Black Prince. In 1374 the Carys became Lords of the Manor. They would be in and out of the estate for the next 300 years. This lack of consistency was due mainly to the fact that the unfortunate Carys, when it came to big political decisions, had the unenviable knack of always backing the wrong horse. If they didn't lose their heads on every occasion, it certainly cost them dearly.

[2] A brochure was produced to advertise the proposed village. Twenty thatched and limewashed buildings were originally envisaged for design by Lutyens. The inn, its garden steps and signpost (itself designed by Dame Laura Knight), and the red telephone box of 1935 are all listed 'buildings'. In 1946, The Prudential Assurance Company bought the village from the Trust. The press at the time laid into Torquay Corporation ridiculing the lack of initiative shown since their acquisition from the Mallocks. The BBC led with the headline 'Thank heaven something has happened to preserve Cockington from Torquay'.

8
ANSTEY'S COVE

First Love

Turning up the hill towards Babbacombe from Torquay harbour, the road starts to wind between the sumptuous Italianate villas of the Warberries, many of them lying back from the road and hidden by trees. After a few minutes, the entrance to the Palace Hotel appears on the right. Originally named Bishopstowe, it was built in 1841 by the Bishop of Exeter, great-uncle of the novelist, Eden Phillpotts, the one-time mentor of the young Agatha Christie. The picturesque villa, that has since been lost under countless extensions and modifications, has become, in Pevsner's words, an 'unprepossessing monster', a situation not helped by being painted a rather dubious shade of green.

Immediately after the hotel, a delightful narrow lane drops down under arches past the hotel grounds to a car park above the cove.

A popular postcard of Agatha's time introduces the multi-talented 'Thomas'. It shows a sign at the top of the path leading down to Anstey's Cove, listing the facilities offered by the refreshment hut down at the water's edge:

> *Picnics supplied with hot water and tea,*
> *At a nice little house down by the sea,*
> *Fresh crabs and lobster every day,*
> *Salmon peel, sometimes Red Mullet and Grey*
> *The neatest of pleasure boats let out on hire,*
> *Fishing tackle as good as you can desire,*
> *Bathing machines for ladies are kept,*
> *With towels and gowns all quite correct,*
> *Thomas is the man who provides everything,*
> *And also teaches young people to swim.*

(Left) The path leading down to Anstey's Cove

(Right) The cove from the car park

Picnics at the time were obviously quite lavish affairs, in keeping with the household menus mentioned in Agatha's autobiography.

In her youth, Anstey's Cove was especially popular for the rather daring midnight picnic (it is not clear whether Thomas stayed open late for these). Agatha refers to one such 'moonlight picnic' where she sat apart on a rock, looking out to sea and holding hands with her sweetheart of the time, a certain Amyas, whom she had met during a local amateur production at Cockington Court.

Early postcards emphasized the romance of Anstey's Cove

One could say that Agatha certainly went for high-flying men. Archie, as we know, was a fighter ace in the First World War (she tells how she longed to be able to wear his St Stanislaus medal at parties). Amyas was a pilot, too. However, Amyas Eden Borton, CB, CMG, DSO, AFC, MiD put even Archie in the shade. Popularly known as 'Biffy', some say that he is responsible for coining the popular name for anti-aircraft fire of the time, 'Archie' through his habit of shouting the words of a popular song of the period, 'Archibald, Certainly Not' as he attempted to dodge the enemy shells. Coincidence or wounded pride?

In a rather touching passage of her autobiography, Agatha recounts that, later in life, when Amyas had become no less than an Air Vice-Marshall, he still asked after her and wished to meet her. Agatha was sixty by that time, and she refused. Was it female vanity – being no longer a slim, young girl? Maybe there were feelings that had not died? Or, more probably, she simply did not wish to destroy a beautiful memory. She did, however, make use of the name Amyas for one of her characters in *Five Little Pigs*. Amyas, who passed away in 1969, would surely have appreciated the compliment.

'On a rock looking out to sea'

    Early postcards reveal that very little has changed since then, apart from the lack of bathing machines. The path descends steeply down the wooded valley. And yes, you can still identify the rock looking out to sea where the young couple sat.

    If it's a nice day then it's more than likely there is a yacht anchored in the cove. The location is once again an 'in' picnic place – these days for the not-quite-as young-as-they-once-were, local 'jet' set.

    The Victorians were less interested in the amazing geology of the area than they were in the quality of the stone to be quarried here.[1] It would provide the marble not only for fireplaces, pillars, floors and steps, but also inkstands and candlesticks, for the luxury villas springing up all around on the hills surrounding Torquay at that time.

AGATHA CHRISTIE'S DEVON

A yacht moored in the cove

Long quarry

The Bishop's Walk

For health and safety reasons, the beach adjacent to Anstey's, Redgate, is no longer accessible from the cliffs of Wall's Hill, via rather precarious steps, as it was when I was a teenager during the 70s (when summers really were summers and not tepid, never-ending monsoons). However, I can see that the lure of a wrasse or pollack still manages to fuddle the mind of clearly vertigo-exempt anglers, enticing them to scramble down the near-vertical rock-face in search of their precious quarry.

Looking at the cove, its location carefully hidden by cliffs and vegetation, you can understand why it was popular amongst smugglers. In 1851, the magistrates court in Torquay records one such episode where coastguards surprised some forty to fifty people bearing barrels of strong foreign spirits.

The clandestine activity was still going on in the late 1980s when Customs and Excise officers sprang a trap one night on a converted trawler which had slipped into the cove and started to unload her cargo of cannabis resin – 70 bales with a market value of over £4million pounds.

Let's return to our friend, Bishop Phillpotts. The Bishop appreciated this stretch of coastline so much that he even had a pathway cut around the cliff so that he could wander down from his palace after lunch, enjoy his constitutional and take in the marvellous vistas while mulling over his next sermon.[2] The path, The Bishop's Walk, is still there, much more wooded than in past times and positively overgrown in its further reaches. The walk ends, somewhat abruptly and disappointingly, amid nettles, brambles and breeze blocks, practically in someone's garage, off Ilsham Marine Drive.

ANSTEY'S COVE

The Bishop's Walk in 1908

Anyway, at least today as I explore, the sun is still shining. From here it's a ten-minute walk back to the car park, admiring along the way the mansions that dot the lower reaches of this, Torbay's answer to Beverley Hills. A chance to reflect on how the 'other half' lives.

NOTES

[1] What strikes one immediately on descending towards the cove is the unusual spike of rock jutting up from the spit of land extending into the sea. As one gets closer, the afternoon sun is picking up the wonderful pink-veined hues of the cliff walls. Geologists among you will have recognised immediately that they are facing a fine example of a stromatoporid reef dating back some 400 million years – a time when this area was home to Caribbean-type islands which emerged from warm seas more or less where Torquay is now. It is these areas so rich in geological heritage, present and visible all around the bay, that have lead to Torbay recently being made a World Geo Park site.

[2] Our Edwardian commentator gets somewhat carried away and has it 'clinging to the precipitous side of the cliff, hanging at a dizzy height above a dozen seething chasms' making it sound more like the Paseo del Rey in the ravines above Malaga rather than Torbay. It does afford, nevertheless, when you manage to get a look through the trees, some fine views of the coastline especially towards Hope's Nose from Black Head (geologists – basaltic igneous intrusion).

(Left) Along Bishop's Walk

(Below) Hope's Nose from the Bishop's Walk

9
THE PAVILION

A Proposal

Today I want to find out where the photographers of Edwardian postcards took those views down towards the Pavilion, with the harbour in the background. The Pavilion is where Agatha Miller took her first steps towards her transformation into Agatha Christie, one of the most famous names in the world. The autobiography is quite clear about the matter -Archibald Christie proposed to Agatha Miller at Ashfield in the music room after a concert at the Pavilion. History, however, has decided otherwise – a proposal during a Wagner concert is much more stirring stuff – and so the story has stuck.

After walking across Waldon Hill a flight of steps begins its precipitous descent towards the harbour.[1] And here is the little terrace where so many of the early cards were snapped from. The pavilion is directly below, and there, where the adjoining car park is now, were the coal stores where ships would unload their cargoes of fuel for the villas of Torquay.

The steps continue at a gentler gradient to the left; the back of the Torbay Hotel is in front of you. It is at this point that we are presented with a one-off sight straight out of García Márquez's *Cien Años de Soledad*. A massive bush of ivy in flower is covered by tens upon tens upon tens of fluttering Red Admiral butterflies, dancing in the sun.

You pass down in front of the red-shuttered Rock House where Gladstone used to stay. The steps finish at ground level in a rather shabby alley which, judging by the evidence, is clearly frequented by people spilling out from the local bars. We climb

View down towards the Pavilion

The Pavilion from Vane Hill

again up the metal steps to the bridge crossing the road towards the pavilion. The bridge forms part of the aesthetically and financially unfortunate 'Winter Gardens' – not a name, as we shall see, that brings much good luck around these parts.

The springy span affords a good head-on view of the Pavilion. It really is a lovely building, reminiscent of Brighton – a delightfully frivolous structure of cream and green Doulton faience and art deco ironwork.

People were worried at the time about the lack of entertainment in Torquay. The Assembly rooms were only really suitable for organised balls, The Winter Gardens Crystal Palace in Torwood Street had flopped, been dismantled and shipped off to Great Yarmouth in 1903.

AGATHA CHRISTIE'S DEVON

(Left) A delightfully frivolous structure

(Centre) The front of the Pavilion

(Right) The Pavilion from St John's Church

An old postcard from 1918. The copper roof of the Pavilion has yet to turn green

A council meeting at the time came to the conclusion that 'Torquay gets duller and duller by the year, and that something must be done to re-establish the town as the best and finest resort of the English coast.' (Even today it sounds unrefreshingly familiar). After much discussion the present site was decided upon. It was already being nicknamed the House of Pleasure. It would be interesting to discover whether the location right opposite the entrance to St John's Church was to cock a snook at authority, or whether the Church wanted it placed there so revelers could feel a pang of guilt as they left.

It was opened on Saturday 17 August 1912. The central dome is surmounted by a full-size figure of 'Britannia' in copper, with two smaller domes surmounted by copper figures of Mercury. The interior was decorated by three trucks of exotic plants – still to be seen in the photographs on display inside. There were also tree ferns brought in from New Zealand. The Pavilion became the place to be seen at the time.

A resident 25-piece orchestra was set up under the directorship of Basil Cameron. Interestingly enough, at that time he was going under the name of Basil Hindenberg, presumably hoping that the teutonic appelation would bring him more work. He hastily (other families did the same), reverted to his more English sounding name at the outbreak of Great War. He soon established the Pavilion's reputation, especially with his series of Wagner concerts, a composer much in vogue at the time.

On 30 April 1930 a four-day music festival took place with renowned guest conductors, Sir Henry Wood and Sir Edward Elgar. The Pavilion also appears around this time in the rather

implausible Unbreakable Alibi in *Partners in Crime*). A little known actor, Harold Pinter, did a six-month season in 1957, including three plays by Agatha Christie.

Incredibly, the building only just avoided being demolished thanks to the intervention of a local preservation group. There were still great concerts here when I was an adolescent – I remember David Bowie and Ten Years After appearing. It later became an ice rink, and now rather sadly it houses a collection of souvenir and novelty shops.

(Left) Britannia

(Centre) Britannia holding balloon

(Right) Mercury

* * * * * *

Agatha Christie had met Archibald Christie at a ball at Ugbrooke House near Exeter, the home of Lord and Lady Clifford. She had been invited by family friends to stay with them in Chudleigh and attend the ball. Another friend had told her to look out for Christie: 'He's a good dancer'.

Archie was not backward in coming forward. She noted his interesting turned-up nose and his careless confidence. He, too, had been told presumably by the same friend to look out for Agatha. They danced and he lived up to his reputation; and then they danced again, and again.

Here Agatha's chronology – never a strength – goes a bit awry on a number of points. The autobiography has Archie turning up 'within a week' at Ashfield, with the rather lame, but charming, excuse that as he had had to come to Torquay on his motorbike anyway, he thought he had better look her up. Yet we have it on reliable authority that the ball took place on 12 October 1912. This in fact rings true as Agatha herself admits she is worried that he might not even remember what she looked like. Did she speed things up to increase Archie's interest for her in her readers' eyes?

Concerts at the Pavilion, including Wagner

The Pavilion, with concerts at 3pm and 8pm being advertised.

Her mother obviously took to him because he is invited to stay to dinner. We find out that they had cold turkey left over from Xmas – which puts the date, in an era without fridges, at not much past 27 December. We read that over the next ten days he kept turning up unexpectedly. She asks him if he would like to go to a Wagnerian concert due to take place in four or five days time at the Pavilion in Torquay. The concert takes place on the 4 January so the ten days must have been more like two days. Maybe now she wants to underplay the whirlwind, if not hurricane, nature of the romance once it got going, fuelled just as much by her invitations as his at this point.

Before the concert takes place they go to a New Year's Ball. Here she notices for the first time that Archie has the 'sick sheep look' about him. He is not speaking and seems almost in a trance. This behaviour, she has learned from previous experiences, means that he 'has got it badly'. She was fond of this theory, so much so that it even gets the run out in one of the novels, *The Pale Horse*.

A quick visit to Torquay library provides a few more details about the day. The *Torquay Times*, of Friday, 3 January 1913, carries at the top of the front page the news of a Wagner concert, under the direction of Basil Hindenberg, with the famous soloist, Madame Blanche Marchesi, prima donna of Covent Garden. The concert was set for Saturday 4 January at 3 pm. Highlight of the afternoon was Madame Blanche's rendition of the Liebstod from 'Tristan und Isolde'.

This emotionally super-charged work, dealing as it does with adultery and powerful sexual feelings was already known to Agatha. She remembers vividly in her autobiography seeing the opera with her sister Madge in London. She recalls the dying moments of the opera as Isolde touches Tristan's lips with hers and falls suddenly across his body. Every night afterwards as she fell asleep she would turn this scene over and over in her mind.

THE PAVILION

Stylish interior decoration

The skylight

It is not clear whether Archie knew what he was letting himself in for. The music certainly worked its effect. The couple walked back up the hill to Ashfield after the concert. You can imagine Archie, even quieter than usual, waiting for the right moment to ask. Agatha perhaps inquires if he is feeling all right – perhaps he hadn't liked the concert? They go up to the schoolroom and Archie bursts out desperately, fiercely, furiously that she has to marry him. She tells him that it is impossible, that she is already engaged to Reggie. He brushes this aside – telling her she will have to break it off.

Agatha makes more token protests and Archie leaves (on his not so trusty, spluttering bike), slightly unsure of whether his proposal has been accepted. There was, however, no need to worry – Agatha, in her own mind, had decided instantly.

NOTES

[1] Leaving the car park outside Torquay Tennis Club, we strike out for Rock Walk, the sub-tropically planted pathway, built along the side of the cliff between Torquay harbour and Abbey Sands when the Princess Gardens were built in 1894. Unfortunately, the recent concerns over the stability of the rock face mean that the way is closed. A steep flight of steps leads up to Warren Road and we find ourselves following the old Fisherman's, or Ladybird walk over Walden Hill – the only way to get from Tor Quay to Abbey meadows before the construction of the Torbay Road in 1840. Ellis in his *History of Torquay* tells us that at the beginning of the nineteenth century the only construction on Walden Hill was a summer house where in 1806 the Princess of Wales took of refreshment. A tablet was of course placed there to commemorate this momentous event – she apparently had found solace there during a very public (newspapers never change through the centuries) 'private' crisis. Ellis mentions that a fragment of this tablet bearing the the words 'favored cell' is embedded in the wall of the steps about half way up. And so it is, still there after all this time.

Once at the top, the empty shell of an elegant Victorian villa catches the eye. Could it be that it is has been earmarked for restoration rather than demolition? It would be a step in the right direction. The 60s and 70s saw the demolition of many a villa and their replacement with 'state-of-the art blocks' Unfortunately they completely desecrated the skyline and one's sense of aesthetics in the process.

Lytton Towers, for example, stands near the site of the villa of the writer, Bulmer-Lytton. His *Last Days of Pompeii* was one of the great reads of mid-century Victorian England. The apartment blocks are popularly known as the Pagodas for obvious reasons. Unfortunately, they are spectacularly lacking in grace, delicacy and balance.

The Pavilion seen from Haldon Pier

10
THE GRAND HOTEL

A brief Honeymoon

We have all had, when children, places that filled us with fear – houses we didn't want to walk past, inhabited by terrifying creations, more often than not, of our own imaginings. For Agatha Christie, it was Corbyn Head. This red sandstone headland has had several arches and stacks that have disappeared, eroded by the waves, since I was a child. The action of the sea has also created caves where Agatha's particular bogeyman, or rather bogeywoman, known as the 'Mad Elder Sister', resided.

It would seem that Agatha's older siblings, Madge and Monty, were not averse to scaring their little sister half out of her wits when they had nothing better to do. Monty, with his penchant for taking pot-shots at the neighbours, would seem a possible candidate for the origin of her 'Gunman' nightmares. And there was absolutely no doubt as to the provenance of her other pet terror who would turn up, from time to time, at the house. The 'Mad Elder Sister' was 'physically indistinguishable' from her sister Madge, but with a sinister, sickly-sweet, Hammer-House-of-Horror voice. She would make her way up from her cavern in the cliff to frighten the life out of Agatha. In typical older-sister style, Madge, when caught, justifies all to her mother with a 'Anyway, she asked me to do it.' retort. The caves of Corbyn Head would make a brief cameo appearance in that repository of childhood memories, *The Postern of Fate*.

The Grand from Princess Gardens

The Grand Hotel stands a little back from this promontory, overlooking the bay.

Built in 1881, it started out life as the Great Western Hotel. It was a homely-looking, modest affair with 12 bedrooms. The main carriage entrance was, as today, at the rear looking towards Torquay station. The hotel was closed in 1908 for a complete renovation. On reopening it became the Grand Hotel.

Rivalry between Grand and Imperial is clear from ads placed in the *Torquay Times*. The Imperial was the 'Premier Hotel in Torquay'. The Grand retorted that it was 'The Only Modern

THE GRAND HOTEL

The facade, 1906

(Left) The Grand seen from Torquay Station in an Edwardian postcard

(Right) The modern block with its subtle curves

First-Class Hotel' on the bay. The Imperial – 'Position unequalled on the South Coast.' The Grand – 'Occupies without doubt the best and most convenient position.' Both claimed south-facing aspects (I'll leave the reader to make up their minds regarding who was telling the truth). However, when the Imperial played its trump card 'Patronage by English and Continental Royal Families', the Grand could only limply respond with 'emergency iron staircases from each floor.'

The Grand has changed little outwardly since 1908. The modern apartment block was built next door in 1972. It is probably the most successful of modern interventions in the bay. Refreshingly minimalist, with the most subtle of curves, it even manages to compliment its stately neighbour.

Unlike Corbyn Head, the hotel has only positive connotations for Agatha, being the place chosen by the newly-wed Christies for their one-night, wartime honeymoon.

The façade today

They were married in Clifton, Bristol on 24 December 1914 during one of Archie's leaves. Agatha, when she wanted, could be every bit as impulsive as her mother, whom she rang to tell what had happened only after a hastily arranged ceremony with a scrambled search for witnesses.

It is not hard to imagine her excitement – the thrill of doing something you know is what you want whatever anyone else may say. Agatha has waited all her life to find Mr Right. Here she is, in the packed compartment of the train from Bristol to Torquay, sitting next to the dashing Archibald Christie. He was tall, athletic, strikingly good-looking with his central

Elegance personified

parting. He had just had his photo in the *London Illustrated News*, the article entitled 'Some Heroes of our Royal Flying Corps'. He was not just a pilot – exotic enough in itself – he was a fighter ace: 'Lieutenant A Christie, mentioned in dispatches October 8 1914'.

And now she was Mrs Christie. It was the night before Christmas. It is fairy-tale stuff.

Not that the months since the engagement had been all smooth sailing. She, like others, had had to make the age-old choice between security and excitement.

Reggie, to whom she had been engaged when she met Archie had made her feel safe. She had been happy and peaceful with him. They had a good understanding. They shared the same interests and wanted the same things. But there was no spark. She mentioned on occasions that something in her temperament made her kick out against situations that were too right or too perfect. Life with Reggie could have become, well, boring. I don't think it is unfair to say that years later, when she came to remarry, Max Mallowan represented the Reggie-version of married life.

Archie, on the other hand, was the high-risk, exciting option. She was fascinated by the fact that they were so different. It was the classic case of opposites attracting. They were, in her words, 'poles apart' in the way they reacted to things. She writes in the autobiography, (somewhat ominously with hindsight), that she was in love with a stranger.

In the past year they had fallen out, had moments of lucidity and broken up only to get back together again unable to bear the thought of not being with each other.

All the warning signs were there, but they were young, desperate and in love.

In some moments, she writes that she had the feeling that she was getting out of her depth and wanted to get back to the safety of the shore.

But she could not *not* go on. She knew and accepted that for everything you love you often have to pay some price and that if you love you may suffer. But neither she, nor Archie, nor anyone, knew at that moment how great that suffering would eventually prove to be.

The tower

The fact was she was in love – and, who knows, it might well have worked. Certainly, she would never have forgiven herself if she had never given it a try.

There had been many options for the honeymoon hotel. The Grand perhaps wasn't as grand as the Imperial, but it had just been refurbished and they had to think about the money, too.

More importantly, for the hours-old couple, impatient to start their marital union together, the fact that they could just walk out of the station straight into conjugal life made it the perfect choice.

But not all was perfect – the hardest thing of all that night was that within 48 hours Archie would have to make his way back to No.3 Squadron at Larkhill and rejoin the war.

There is an Agatha Christie suite at The Grand, but the exact room she stayed in is not known

11
TORQUAY HOSPITAL

Poirot is born

The old Torquay Hospital is an imposing building, its sheer walls of granite tower skywards. It could, with the right illumination: some flickering flashes of lightning, some claps of thunder, come straight out of a Gothic thriller.

Standing in front of the building, I wanted to pinpoint the room where Agatha's career had started – for it was here that she first put pen to paper to produce *The Mysterious Affair at Styles*. There were no plans indicating original rooms available. I had one passage from the autobiography to go on. One night the novice nurse lay awake in bed at home, worrying that maybe she had put the wrong substance in a batch of ointments. She could stand it no longer, got dressed and went back down to the hospital. She says that she did not have to walk through the ward, since the staircase to the dispensary was outside it.

The site manager (the building is being converted into flats), was of great help to me. We narrowed it down to one of the four central windows on the first floor but that was as far as we could get. Perhaps it's just as well. If we had identified it, future owners might not have appreciated groups of Japanese Agatha fans taking photos in front of their idol's shrine.

The hospital had had modest beginnings in 1844 when three rooms were acquired in Union Street for use as a public dispensary.

The foundation stone of the new hospital in Trematon Avenue was laid in August 1850 by Prince Peter of Oldenburg, one of the steady stream of Russian nobility passing through the resort in that era. By Christie's time, it had a fever ward, a children's ward, an operating theatre, even a lift, though electric light wouldn't arrive till after the Great War.

At the outbreak of war, to cope with the wounded at the front, beds were increased from 64 to 120 and then again to 130 in 1916. During the war, 2293 such soldiers were treated on the wards. Incredibly only 15 of those soldiers died – a testament to the skill and dedication of the doctors and nurses involved.

Following in the footsteps of her Great Grandfather's wife, Agatha Christie began her training as a nurse as soon as she heard that the country had entered the conflict. Her first job

Straight out of a Gothic thriller!

as part of the recently-formed VAD (Voluntary Aid Detachment) was at the Town Hall in Castle Circus which had been converted into a field hospital. She started as a ward-maid with basic cleaning duties. Within five days she had been promoted to nurse. Many who had been taken on for this job had not realised the harsh realities of the situation. Agatha, however, despite the bed-pans, the vomit, the lice, festering wounds and amputations, took to it immediately. She got on well with the soldiers – even, as she recalls, writing love-letters, sometimes in triplicate to three different girls, for those who could not write.

A bad bout of flu kept her at home for several weeks. When she returned, she found that she had been transferred to a new department – the dispensary in the hospital in Union Street. It was decided she would study, while working, for the qualification of Apothecary's Assistant.[1]

She received instruction for the exam in the hospital and also from a chemist in his shop in Torquay. This was the infamous 'Mr P' who, because of the feeling of power it gave him, would habitually carry around with him in his pocket a lump of curare

The garden gifted to the hospital in 1897

A view looking up Union Street, 1905

AGATHA CHRISTIE'S DEVON

A postcard on which a wounded soldier indicates his ward with an arrow. He signs off, 'Happy Christmas and may the New Year bring us peace', 23 Dec 1917.

Former site of Mr P's chemist's shop in Torre

(a deadly South American arrow poison).[2] The sinister Mr P stayed in her mind and more than 50 years later would inspire the novel *The Pale Horse*. She went on to pass the three-part exam in chemistry, *materia medica* and compounding with the mediocre score of 50 per cent. Perhaps the only part which really interested her was poisons. And her mind was on other things

Working in the dispensary and surrounded by pestles, mortars, flasks, bunsens, and countless blue and green phials of deadly compounds, Agatha began to hatch the embryonic ideas for her first detective novel. Now she had time on her hands compared to the intensive nursing she had been doing before – time to think about the characters of her book. Time to think about the victim, the murderer, the motive. Time to think about who, why when and where. Sitting for long hours in the dispensary, one thing crystallized in her mind fairly quickly and that was the 'how'. Poison. Poison was going to be a life-long affair for her. She is reputed to have said 'Give me a bottle of poison and I will construct the perfect crime'. Over half her works have poisoning as their theme – cyanide, statistically, is her favourite way of despatching her victims. Then there is also arsenic, taxine, thallium, digitoxin adrenaline, novocaine, trinitrine, aconite, stropanthin, phosphorus, and finally, her choice for her first novel -*The Mysterious Affair at Styles* – strychnine.

Not surprisingly, in the first book, she drew heavily on her own experience. There are several incidents in the autobiography that appear in the novel. There were many Belgian refugees in Torre at the time. The selection of the Belgian detective, Hercule Poirot gave her the chance to use her knowledge of French she had acquired in France and with her lady's maid during her unorthodox education. The character Cynthia Murdoch is based on her own situation. She first appears in her VAD uniform, is working in the dispensary – her sanctum – studying for her Apothecary's Certificate at the Red Cross Hospital in Tadminster. And, is it my imagination, or does the plan of the Torquay hospital I have been looking at bear more than a passing resemblance to the layout of the building in the novel?

Her comments on the relationships in the novel expressed her own opinions and fears, The scene of the refused proposal is straight out of her own experience of suitors. Her knowledge of poisons, their tastes and how these tastes could be camouflaged were the direct result of her work at the hospital and her studies for the Apothecaries exam. Later Agatha was to say that she was most flattered by a review the book received from *The Pharmaceutical Journal* which praised the author's knowledge of poisons.

There are two things in *The Mysterious Affair at Styles* that would change in future works, both relating to Christie's use of her own experiences.

First, and this is something she has been criticised for, was her use of her expert knowledge relating to poisons. The details about crystallisation, about the combination of narcotics with poisons – these were things that the layman could not possibly be privy to – thus making it impossible for the ordinary reader to solve the mystery. In a way, for the purists, she had broken one of the unwritten rules of crime fiction.

The other was the graphic description of death – 'tetanic' in character, as Dr Bauerstein describes it. The terrible convulsions, the arching of the body, the strangled voice – it was almost as if she had witnessed the scene in real life.

The Dispensary at Torquay Hospital, 1928

She had in fact. The clenching of the muscles of the mouth and jaw, giving the appearance of a grin – the *risus sardonicus in extremis* – she had experienced it at first hand. It is there in a throw-away line of the autobiography. One of her first soldiers at the hospital had died of tetanus – she had been deeply shocked by it. Had she gone home that night and written down her terrible experience? Probably she didn't need to – so deeply was it etched into her memory.

Perhaps she felt she had overstepped the mark. Whatever the reason, from now on death would take place off-stage, would be respected and sterilised – all that we have come to expect, in short, from the Queen of Crime.

Her stories are far from gruesome. In fact, most people find reading them quite calming. We are light years away from Patricia Cornwell's graphically described autopsies. When a murder does occur it takes place generally well out of sight. *Ne coram publico Medea pueros trucidet*, as Max Mallowan wrote, quoting Horace in true classical scholar style.

In the 'raid libraries' set up during the blitz, detective novels were the most frequently requested and Agatha Christie topped the list. People found, when all around was chaos and destruction, the novels cosy and comforting. A fifty-year-old widow confessed: 'I like to have to concentrate. The suspects, and working it all out – you know – it soothes your nerves.' Jewish inmates even did a production of 'And Then There Were None' at Buchenwald Concentration Camp.

At one point – in *Hercule Poirot's Christmas* – after her brother-in-law had complained that the murders were becoming too tame, she promised to make things more gory, more violent with loads of blood. She was of course pulling his leg. Sure there is a sentence which says that there was a great pool of blood near the body but that is it. And even then, that blood… but I mustn't give the game away.

Agatha Christie novels are more like intricate puzzles. Identifying the red herrings, working out possible motives is like doing crosswords or literary sudokus – the things she liked doing so much in her free time. The novels, far from agitating, relax and calm the mind. And this I think was why deep down Agatha Christie, herself, took up writing. Consider the situation. Her fiance had just left for the war. He was in the Flying Corps – a newly formed untested unit. Even the planes were largely untested in combat situations. There was every probability that he wouldn't come back.

Writing took her mind off this, concentrated her imagination and relaxed her. When she wrote she was mistress of her emotions. Writing, for someone who feared loss of control more than anything, became like a drug. Luckily for murder mystery junkies around the world, it would prove to be a life-long addiction.

NOTES

1. Medicine was becoming more sophisticated and prescriptions more complicated and this work could no longer be done satisfactorily by unqualified staff. That more women were now obtaining this exam was due to the work of the Society for Promoting the Employment of Women (a somewhat unfortunate acronym) who had turned their attention in the second half of the nineteenth century to new possible trades for women. The example of Florence Nightingale in the Crimea had also done a lot to further this.

2. Curare is made from bark which if injected into the bloodstream kills in minutes by paralysing the muscles needed to breathe, leaving the victim completey lucid in his agony, with heart still beating normally yet unable to get any air. However, if ingested its large molecules cannot pass through the stomach lining and is thus harmless. Which is just as well, otherwise the natives of the Amazon would not be able to eat the animals they had killed using the poison.

12
THE MOORLAND HOTEL, HAYTOR, DARTMOOR

Murder in the Heather

From Torbay, you can see Haytor on the skyline. In fact, you can see it from almost all over South Devon: from Shaldon at the mouth of the Teign, to Start Point at the end of Slapton Bay. Although at 454 metres it is not the highest tor on the moor, it is by far and away the most visible.

Haytor (left) and Saddle Tor

Haytor with ponies

Haytor and the surrounding countryside were to play a key role in the launch of Agatha Christie's literary career. She had started to plan her first novel in her head and was putting down the ideas on paper. She was finding it difficult, however, to make all the pieces needed to puzzle the reader fit seamlessly into the jigsaw. Not surprisingly, she found it harder to concentrate on more mundane tasks. She knitted the sleeve all wrong on her Granny's cardigan. Letters supposed to be sent to X went to Y. Her frustration increased. She had reached, as Poirot would have put it, *une impasse*.

At this point her mother, with great foresight, sensitivity and judgment, stepped in. Why not take a fortnight off, go away, alone, with no distractions and break the back of the book? Agatha realised it was a brilliant idea and mother knew the perfect location – Dartmoor. She booked herself into a room at the Moorland Hotel, Haytor

She had come up here as a child for picnics. There was nothing better than a good picnic in the Christie household. When her father was alive, they had rented a place on the moors one summer to escape the heat of Torquay. This is where she would take her mother on trips when she first acquired her bull-nosed Morris. She would also bring Max up here for a rain-soaked day out. Even Hercule Poirot would take himself off to Spitchwick for a *pique-nique* in *Evil Under the Sun*.

I was lucky enough, when browsing in a wonderful second hand bookshop just opposite the old hospital, to find a Ward Lock *Guide to Dartmoor* of that very year – 1916.

Advertisements from Ward Lock's Guide to Dartmoor, *1916*

It's the ads that give you the best feel for the period. There are names still famous today, but with slightly different slants. Cadbury's Chocolate comes with an endorsement from *The Medical Magazine*. Vaseline lists amongst its multifarious uses, the ability to give 'a Healthy and Glossy appearance to the Hair'. Others sadly are no longer with us – Mrs *Beeton's Household Management* – half-calf or half-morocco binding – with its chapters on Menus and Menu Making, Trussing and Carving, and, Mistress and Servant. Then there is 'Valet – the self-stropping safety razor'; 'Argonaut original straw hat polish – beware of imitations'; and my personal favourite, Brands meat lozenges for Tourists, athletes and invalids – 'a meal in your vest pocket'.

And, there, first in the directory of hotels and boarding establishments is The Moorland Hotel. 'The nearest hotel to Haytor Rock. 1100 feet above the sea, on the far-famed Dartmoor, commanding extensive views of the surrounding country', while 'the sea is easily discernible in the distance at Teignmouth and Tor Bay from all front windows'. The autobiography is not so flattering in its description: 'large and dreary'.

I now know too that the hotel had electric light, perfect sanitation, excellent cuisine, and good fox and otter hunting. Agatha would have caught a train from Torre, five minutes from Ashfield, on the Teign Valley line, alighting at Bovey Tracey station. From here she would have been whisked to her destination by one of the fleet of motors from the hotel (at which point, after travel, there would have been nothing more refreshing than a bath with Wright's coal tar soap!). If on the other hand our authoress-to-be were running late then she could call Mrs Hellier, the proprietor, on '7 Haytor Vale' to advise. A single room was 2 shillings and 6 sixpence for the night and full board started at 63 shillings a week.

Advertisement for The Moorland Hotel from Ward Lock's Guide to Dartmoor, *1916*

Widecombe-in-the-Moor

(Above) The road to Islington

(Centre) The Rock Inn, Haytor Vale

(Right) Mist comes down over the moor

The Moorland Hotel, Haytor Vale

Anyway it served its purpose. Agatha would work every morning till lunch – 'till my hand ached' – then eat and strike out on her own across country. She wanted to avoid the crowds that clustered around the tor. It would seem that back in 1916 things were pretty much as they are now – most of the visitors to Haytor limit their incursion on to the moor to walking up to the tor, and afterwards buying an ice-cream at the bottom to reward their efforts, and then perhaps drive on to Widecombe-in-the-Moor for a cup of tea and a scone.

She writes how she loved the tors and heather, and while she walked she would go over the dialogue in the book to herself. It is in these surroundings that Hercule Poirot first uttered his now legendary quips and asides.

I turn off towards Ilsington. A tree-lined avenue leads to the village which has a fine looking church. The road starts to climb into the mist. Trees give way to bracken. We pass the Rock Inn and adjacent cottages, built for the workers in Haytor granite quarries in the 1800s. The inn, famous for its hospitality and fine food, and is mentioned in the *Michelin Guide* 2008.

Then it's a left turn over the cattle grid and we are on to the moor proper. The mist is even thicker. Haytor is invisible, and you can barely make out the edge of the road. Agatha wouldn't have been walking today.

I am welcomed to the Moorland Hotel by the owner, Keith, who, seeing my camera, congratulates me on my choice of day. He leaves me to wander round the garden and take a few pictures. What strikes one immediately, compared with photos from the past, is the abundance

of trees. It has been the same in all the locations I have visited – The Lincombes, Anstey's Cove, Greenway. Perhaps the use of trees for fuel in the past restricted the growth of woodland, but it is a noticeable difference from the landscape Agatha would have known.

An aging croquet set reminds me of how Agatha might have passed an idle half hour if she had one. I suspect she didn't. There is a circular pool in the corner of the garden, with a sign by the side of it, 'Danger'. There must be a murder mystery there somewhere. There is also a curious church altar in the corner of the garden

I make my way back inside to see if Keith has any stories to tell me.

It seems a Mr John Hellier, a gentleman in the quarrying business, had married a certain Lucy Lee. When he died in 1892 she built the hotel in his memory. By 1905 it had 20 bedrooms. The pool was a Victorian plunge pool fed by diverting the nearby River Lemon. Keith is clearly proud of his theory that this was the inspiration for the name of Hercule's super efficient secretary, Miss Lemon.[1]

It wasn't till 1969 that disaster struck the hotel. During an event organised by the local constabulary the hotel caught fire and was totally gutted – including the room Christie had stayed in. The *Express & Echo* ran the story on the front page: 'Dancing PCs flee Devon Hotel

(Left and above) The Moorland Hotel today and how it looked in the 1920s, complete with croquet lawn

(Above) Croquet, my dear?

(Left) The plunge pool fed by the River Lemon

(Right) The view from a bedroom

Fire'. It seems ironic that Superintendent Battle's colleagues, with whom Christie had worked vicariously for so many years, had been indirectly involved in the destruction of yet another piece in the Agatha Christie jigsaw.

The hotel was eventually taken over in 1979 by Sidney Hindle, who had made his fortune with a string of remnant shops in the South West. He refurbished the hotel and most of his makeover still remains. Sidney was eccentric, to say the least, and the décor reflects his personality. The walls are covered with black silk taffeta. The centrepiece of the lounge is a giant chandelier, like a frozen waterfall, three metres across and weighing half a ton. It was originally on the liner QE2. Incongruous is a word that springs to mind. Not surprisingly, the altar in the garden is one of Sidney's ideas, too, bought from an old priory.

The guests leaving on the morning I visited, were all very happy. They were, judging from their attire, seasoned walkers. Forget the décor, that's what this place is all about. You are out there on the moor – Haytor and miles and miles of unspoilt wilderness are literally on the doorstep. It's a hiker's dream come true.

Outside again, the mist has if anything got worse. I unintentionally startle an enormous buff-coloured, swirly-coated heifer which appears out of the gloom. For a hairy moment he has it in his eye to charge the car. I park up and wait for the mist to lift.

Sooner than expected, Haytor reveals itself. It looks like a gigantic remnant thrown from a prehistoric volcano. 'Tor', let me eruditely inform you, is one of those very few Celtic words left in the English language; *Twr* (pronounced Tar) meant tower.

Ten thousand years ago the moorland was heavily wooded. Clearing of the forest for grazing and agriculture by our Stone, Bronze and Iron Age ancestors meant that much of the ancient tree cover disappeared, except for the birch, hawthorn and rowan we find today. I must admit that this open aspect of the moor is what I have always loved since I was a child. There is a distinct difference once you pass over the cattle grid on to the moor, when the trees disappear to be replaced by bracken, gorse and heather.

The decaying vegetation has produced a thick layer of peat. Due to the impervious bedrock, in some places there is more water then vegetable material, and mires form. On days like this they can be extremely dangerous for the unwary walker. The most famous is the fictitious Grimpen Mire of *The Hound of the Baskervilles* by Sir Arthur Conan Doyle, a mystery writer of an earlier age, but one whose works Agatha must have been most familiar with (see Chapter 14). The bottomless depth of these bogs and mires is legendary.

(Previous page) Haytor: like a remnant thrown from a prehistoric volcano

(Left) The Moorland Hotel c.1960

(Below) Gorse and heather beneath Haytor

The fine-grained granite from the quarries at Haytor was much sought after for building. The British Museum and London Bridge were constructed from this stone. It is still possible to visit the quarry to the north-east. If you continue past the tor and then down to the right you will find a beautiful pool, an oasis with abandoned machinery, dragonflies, frogs, waterlilies and the occasional goldfish. The remains of the granite railway built in 1820 to transport the rock down to Stover and then by canal to Teignmouth are still there.

Across the valley stands Hound Tor and beyond that rises the impressive mass of Hamel Down – the High Moor. The window in the mist is already closing again. That will be for another day. I make my way down to the car park. Even Mr Whippy wouldn't be out in this weather, would he?

NOTES
[1] I must admit Keith's theory fits with the way Agatha Christie came up with the names for her characters. I nod admiringly, but still can't mentally place Miss Lemon in *The Mysterious Affair at Styles*. Later I learn that the super-efficient Miss Lemon made her first appearance in *Parker Pyne Investigates* in 1934, and didn't move on to work for Poirot until *Hickory Dickory Dock* in 1955.

Hound Tor with Hamel Down beyond

13
KENTS CAVERN

The Man in the Brown Suit

It would seem that Mrs Tiggy-Winkle, the self-effacing, prickly but loveable, troglodytic, laundry woman, was inspired by Beatrix Potter's visit to Kents Cavern at the end of the 1800s. The entrance to the caves was not the grand affair it is today. It was simply a door let into the cliff face, much like our hedgehog friend's home. It would seem that they also had difficulty getting reception staff to man the entrance judging from the photograph below.

If the first explorer of the caves, Father McEnery, was more of an Indiana Jones-type figure (on one expedition falling through the cave floor and lying unconscious for hours), it was William Pengelly who first brought a scientific approach to the excavations.

We have him to thank that the marble-mad Victorians didn't get their hands on the place and turn the hillside into yet another quarry. He had worked his way up from coastal trading boats in Looe in Cornwall, moved to Torquay to become a teacher, and ended up tutoring the children of royalty. In this respect, it helped that the number of European Royal family members per square mile was reputed to be higher in Torquay at this time than anywhere else on the Continent. Having an enormously influential and rich benefactor, Angela Burdett-Coutts, did him no harm either.

Pengelly and McEnery remembered

The caves were formed around two and a half million years ago as rainwater percolated through fissures in the limestone. Pengelly and his helpers had to dig down through thick calcified layers covering the cave floor in order to uncover the secrets of the cave and its previous occupants.

In the topmost layers they unearthed Roman coins, decorated iron age pottery and

A custodian of the caves in the early days

(Left) The limestone feature known as The Face

(Centre) The In-Between boss

(Right) The Rocky Chamber

The dashing Max Mallowan

The Natural History Society Museum

Bronze Age burial artifacts. Below this they found animal bones of the last Ice Age – reindeer, woolly rhinoceros, mammoth, bears and hyaenas. Bone harpoons, flint spearheads and small hand-axes, dating back as far as 80 000 years also came to light. In the lowest layer, Pengelly found even older hand-axes and bones of cave bears. These were dated to almost half a million years ago. In addition they found remains of cave lions and scimitar cats.

Much later, in 1927, a team of workmen, digging just inside the entrance vestibule, found a piece of human jawbone containing three teeth. It was carbon dated to 31 000 years ago – the oldest known evidence of anatomically modern humans anywhere in North Western Europe.

Pengelly and Darwin had a tough time convincing the public of the true age of the Earth and their theories of evolution. Agatha Christie's father, however, was one of the more enlightened members of the town. 1894 sees him being admitted to the ranks of the Torquay Natural History Society, one of the main financers of work in the caves.

Although no mention is made of it in the autobiography, Agatha would have undoubtedly visited the excavations. Her interest in history and archaeology therefore predated her meeting with Max Mallowan in Iraq. There is, however, apparently no truth in the story that she once admitted that the best thing about being married to an archaeologist is that the older you get the more notice he takes of you.

In *The Man in the Brown Suit*, a fleeting reference is made to the caves which have been

KENTS CAVERN

(Left) Torquay Museum

(Right) The cave business today

Kents Cavern's. A scallop shell holding spaghnum moss dipped in animal fat is used to light the caves

renamed Hampsley's Cavern. In the novel the heroine's father is involved in excavations in a cave which is rich in deposits of the Aurignacian culture. The village of Little Hampsley also has a museum where artifacts and bones of wooly (sic) rhinoceros and cave bear are exhibited. The father catches a chill (the workers in the real caves, too, complained of damp conditions, many contracting rheumatism). Agatha's character is more unfortunate: obviously no longer of importance for the plot, he is dispatched in a rather perfunctory fashion with double pneumonia.

As a tourist attraction Kents Cavern ran into difficulties in the 1980s and as a result new initiatives were implemented (very successfully, it must be said) to attract more visitors, and the owners of the site are now bringing the heritage of the caves to a much wider audience.

Among these initiatives are the staging of 'ghost evenings', with added spirits too (the two main caverns are now fully licensed). A big thing is made of halloween (so much so that it was difficult to get any photos the first time I visited without a pumpkin featuring somewhere in the shot). Visiting Santa in his grotto has also taken on a whole new dimension at Kents Cavern around Christmas time, while it is even possible nowadays to tie the knot amongst the stalactites (hanging down) and stalagmites (sticking up), as the caves are licensed for weddings.

William Pengelly and seventeen friends founded the Torquay Natural History Society in 1844. It is still very active in the town, producing pamphlets, organizing educational visits to the museum and inviting guest speakers to talk.

An interesting lecture was advertised during the 2008 Agatha Christie Festival. Mathew Prichard, Agatha Christie's grandson, was invited to speak about his grandmother and some special tapes he had found…

The Hall at the Museum was packed. I sat with a William Pengelly plaque looking down on me. 'Thorough in All Things' read the inscription.

Mathew explains that during the recent renovation of Greenway House he had come across an old Grundig tape-recorder and boxes of tapes that belonged to his grandmother. After many months of careful restoration the tape-recorder has been made to work again and tonight we will be hearing dictated excerpts which eventually formed Agatha's autobiography.

In the first excerpt she is talking about the play, 'The Mousetrap'. The tape starts up. A disembodied voice is heard against a background of whirrs and clicks (she is starting and stopping the recorder). It's like someone talking to you through a school of porpoises. However, one's ear quickly gets accustomed to filtering out the background noise. Agatha sounds, of course, distinctly upper class, rather like the Queen, only more expressive.

A frisson run through the audience when Mathew talks of 'my grandmother', or we hear Agatha say 'Mathew, my grandson…' and at a later moment when Mathew says 'I never knew my true grandfather'. The last is particularly poignant since Mathew when at Eton contacted his Grandfather, Archie, and they arranged to meet in London. A matter of days before the appointment, Archie collapsed and died.

And now here is that grandson in front of us, rocking slowly back and forth. Of ruddy complexion, grey-haired, with beetling eyebrows, jovial, a lover of fine food perhaps, and, at the moment, beaming – given the present topic, 'The Mousetrap' – like the cat who has decidely got the cream!

As we listen to more excerpts, Agatha's voice speaks volumes about her sense of humour and her modesty (Mathew tells us she refused to become a Dame before her husband, Max, was himself knighted). She is rigorously self-critical when it comes to her writing.

Her shyness – her life-long fear of speaking in public – seems to have disappeared. Mathew reminds us she was alone with her dog when making these tapes. You get the feeling that he, too, is quite shy and probably quite happy to be giving this 'cop-out' lecture as he puts it. The feeling is reinforced later when a lady in the audience compliments him on how good looking he was as a child… at which point he turns a light shade of beetroot.

He tells us how Agatha loved to deceive people – a wonderful summing up of her work laden with its barrels and barrels of red herrings. She based almost everything on her own observations and things that actually happened, either in the newspaper or elsewhere. I notice that on the tapes she pronounces 'Herkewl Poirot' in the English way rather than 'Hercool Poirot'.

The final excerpt is about Ashfield. Although a couple of the front row local dignitaries have nodded off by this point, the Agatha fans are loving every click, crackle and knock.

I was hoping for the passage from the very end of the autobiography when she returns to the place where Ashfield had once stood. This passage, however, is the part where she is steeling herself for the sale of Ashfield so as to buy Greenway. And this is the side of her personality which is less easy to like. Agatha clearly came from a silver-spoon-in-the-mouth background and would probably admit quite openly to being a snob. On the tapes she laments the building of the 'horrible little houses' on the road up to Shiphay – look at them today and you will see what 'little' meant to her. She resented the building of the Grammar School – which blocked her view of the sea. There is a general dissatisfaction with the loss of privileges that the upper classes enjoyed: large houses, servants, a life of leisure – all of which had gone into rapid decline with the passing of the Edwardian period.

However, the fact remains that it is Mathew's grandmother speaking and an emotional bout of coughing at the end shows how much this is moving him. Conscious of the pause, he asks: 'Is this having the same effect on you as it is on me?'

Time for questions. 'How much have you earned from 'The Mousetrap?' is one I feel is too delicate to ask. 'How do you think your grandmother would have felt about the opening of Greenway to the public?' is another question that might appear provocative. Agatha was such a private, modest person, and Greenway was her retreat, her refuge where she became Mrs Mallowan not Agatha Christie. It is unlikely she would have approved.

Instead I ask, 'How do you feel about the opening of Greenway to the public?' Mathew looks at me straight in the eye and says that emptying out the house at first was very difficult (and one is reminded how difficult it was for Agatha to clear her mother's house), but now he wholeheartedly embraced the idea – it will be good to have people back in there he says.

* * * * * *

I am glad that I saw Greenway before the restorers moved in. I'm sure it will look marvellous but it will never again have the stamp that the Mallowans and Hicks had left on the place. They were great collectors and hoarders and to leave it as it was would be too much of a risk with hundreds of visitors passing through it every day. Unless I am very much mistaken, what we shall see will inevitably be a more sanitised version, but an absolute must-see for Christie fans nonetheless.

14
SITTAFORD TOR, CHAGFORD

(Left) The Three Crowns porch; (Right) The Three Crowns sign
(Below) Chagford's famous hardware shop

The Sittaford Mystery

The Three Crowns is in Chagford, opposite the church. Built of sombre local granite, it dates back to the thirteenth century. During the Civil War, the Cavalier poet, Sidney Godolphin, was caught by musket fire during a skirmish and died in the porchway of the inn. His ghost is still said to haunt the Three Crowns, which perhaps suggested to Christie the supernatural element in her novel.

Much of the early part of the novel revolves around the inn, since Sittaford village is cut off by snow. This is where Major Burnaby lodges, after discovering the murdered Captain Trevelyan, unable to return home as the roads are blocked. James Pearson, nephew of the deceased also checks in. As does Charles Enderby, the journalist of the *Daily Wire*. It is in the porchway of the hotel that Burnaby 'explodes' when accosted by the newspaperman. Emily Trefusis turns up; Inspector Narracott, too; and we find out that Evans, the victim's manservant, has married the landlady's daughter. At this point, we only need Uncle Tom Cobley and the party will be complete. It is no wonder that the author refers darkly to 'inbreeding' in these small Dartmoor villages.

When I eventually find a place to park I take a look around. Chagford, of late, has become known as Celebrity Corner, with a whole host of television celebrities having set up house in the vicinity. It's a place worth coming to just to see the famous hardware shop, a labyrinthine Aladdin's cave selling just about everything under the sun, but all with decidedly 'country-style' flavour to it. The wine and cheese stores in the village would not be out of place on Chelsea High Street.

Dodging the Range Rovers I drive out towards Fernworthy, on my way to Sittaford Tor. As I leave Chagford I pass several uncannily convincing, tweed-clad, Miss Marple look-alikes.

I enter the plantation at Fernworthy. At intervals, streams cascade down through the pine forest on their way to join the reservoir. The road comes to an end but there is a gate open and a track leads into the woods. My map shows that there is still quite a walk to the edge of the open moor. There isn't a soul to be seen. I drive slowly up the track.

There's an expanse of stumps where enormous trees have been felled. Morning mist is still in the air. The whole place has an eerie, primeval feel about it. Alongside the wall leading on to the moor, an empty Land Rover and horsebox is parked up. At least, I'm not the only one around.

I've never been here before and you can't actually see where the tor is. I've been told that although in a high position it's not a tower like Haytor or Sharp Tor, rather just a pile of slabs. I'm prepared – I have my Dartmoor Explorer Ordnance Survey map and a compass.

A ruined farmstead allows me to get my bearings. I calculate where the 'invisible' tor should be and strike out straight for it. Mistake! I soon find myself struggling through a terrain consisting of giant tufts of grass interspersed with unseen potholes, sometimes a metre deep. I have got myself into a natural assault course with a fiendish step component which soon has my thigh muscles aching. Overdressed and hot, I can hear my heart beating in my ears. The thought suddenly flashes through my head that if anything happens to me there is no mobile signal – I could lie here for weeks.

This moment of melodrama is soon over, and once past the leat that I should have realised separated me from the Tor, the terrain becomes steeper but easier.

I finally arrive. The tor is only a couple of metres high – one of the giant stones used to be a logan stone (a rock you can stand on and rock back and forth) but no longer.

There is total silence. This is the point that Emily, self-styled sleuth, climbs up to in order to clear her thoughts and take stock of her situation. As Emily says, high up like this one ought

(Left) The approach to Fernworthy

(Centre) A stream feeding into the reservoir

(Above) An eerie scene

Fernworthy forest

(Top) Looking north from Sittaford Tor

(Bottom) The view back to Fernworthy Forest

(Right) Grey Wethers stone circles

Lettaford

to see things better. The view is breathtaking and seemingly limitless, I too, soon find myself lost in my own thoughts…

I begin to make my way down. There is a wall with a well-worn path alongside it running down to the valley floor. I realise that this is the way I should have come up. Over the wall, to the right, stand two large dark stone circles – the Grey Wethers. They seem almost too perfect, every stone upright and exactly spaced. Indeed they are much "restored", the result of nineteenth century intervention. The Victorians had a mania when it came to ancient monuments, and for 'tidying things' up. Fortunately, they made drawings of the state of affairs before the make-over occurred. Legend has it that unfaithful wives were brought to the Grey Wethers to kneel before the great stones to wait for judgement. If the woman was absolved the stones remained standing. If a stone fell, it crushed the unfortunate (though clearly guilty) woman. Most of the stones were found lying on the ground by the Victorian antiquaries…[1]

There are many likely candidates for the village of Sittaford. It was, we are told in the novel, not in a sheltered valley like most moorland settlements, but clinging to the shoulder of the moor below Sittaford Tor. Christie knew the area well. Apart from being an avid picnicker, ten years before she had had to find a cottage on Dartmoor for her ever-more 'eccentric' brother, Monty, who was driving the household at Ashfield mad.

There are many small clusters of cottages in the area that roughly fit the novel's description. Here the lanes run up through a few scattered houses and often comes to an abrupt end at a gate leading on to the moor. One of my favourite candidates for Sittaford – and the name supports this too – is Lettaford. This is reached by one of those narrow lanes where, as you drive further along it, the tufts of grass in the centre become ever more frequent. You start to wonder if the road is ever used at all and if it won't just peter out in a few yards…

And then it does. The situation is right – just on the edge of the moor not far from Sittaford Tor. The Dartmoor longhouses at Lettaford, built of huge granite ashlars, are some of the best preserved of their kind.

As for the inspiration for Sittaford House, my main suspect is Gidleigh Park. The 'Park House' was built in the sixteenth century, and the original road to Gidleigh Castle and church runs through fields to the rear of the house. It stands in a beautiful park overlooking a river. At the beginning of the twentieth century the house was in a bad state of repair and it was purchased in 1925 by an Australian sheep farmer and shipping magnate called Charles Harold Campbell McIlwraith. Agatha's book was published in 1930. She would surely have heard of this new arrival on the scene. She makes the owner of Sittaford House, a certain Captain Trevelyan, a retired naval man. And she would incorporate the Australian connection into the novel, too. We can see how Agatha's mind works – re-arranging ideas, fitting them to her knowledge of the area until they fit her plot. She even throws in, with the convict, a 'quotation' from Conan Doyle's *The Hound of the Baskervilles*.

When it comes to place names, Agatha Christie adores playing games with her readers. More than anything she adapted things as she needed them. Chagford with its Three Crowns was clearly the village that inspired her. However, Sittaford House was physically too close to Chagford for the purposes of the plot. The solution was simple: Chagford became Exhampton,

(Left) Gidleigh Park

(Right) The North Teign river at Gidleigh

which sounds like Okehampton. She gives it a castle which Chagford doesn't have, but Okehampton does – which causes confusion – all the better.

Back on the road that runs from Princetown to Moretonhampstead, I take a left towards Widecombe-in-the-Moor. It's my favourite road on the moor. Everything here tells you to slow down, that nothing that man has created is really important. I sit and wait a good five minutes till a black-faced ram in front of me decides it is time to move off. It wouldn't be right to sound the horn – I am the intruder in his wilderness.

You can understand why Indian ecologist and Ghandi-disciple, Satish Kumar – who once walked 8,000 miles without money across mountains, steppes and snow from Ghandi's grave in New Delhi to the tomb of John F Kennedy to protest in favour of disarmament – has decided to live here.

I pass Grimspound, a wonderfully preserved (and just a little restored) Bronze Age walled settlement, with superb hut circles, hidden high up above the road. Then it's across the narrowest bridge on the moor – Ponsworthy and on to Poundsgate. I have learnt from the author Brian Carter that every ramble-cum-article worth its salt should finish with a pint. And I confess that, like Brian, I am one of those heathens that prefers lager to CAMRA brews.

I know just the place. The Tavistock Inn at Poundsgate serves some of the best food on the moor. The Landlord and the same semi-permanent locals are always there to greet you. A baguette with mushrooms cooked in garlic and red wine with Somerset brie is consumed with a pint of Fosters on a stool at the bar. Perfection!

The Tavistock Inn, Poundsgate

NOTES

[1] More scientifically, considerable quantities of charcoal were found inside the circles showing they were once the site of enormous ritual fires. The south-easterly access of many of the circles points to a possible winter solstice festival. Such circles appear to have been constructed outside village enclosures. Here, they straddle the dip between White Hill and Sittaford Tor suggesting the circles were for the use of communities from both north and south of the valley.

15
THE IMPERIAL HOTEL

Peril at End House, The Body in the Library, Sleeping Murder

The best thing about the Imperial Hotel is the view of the bay. The description of the scene drew forth, from Victorian and Edwardian commentators, the purplest of prose: 'In places, it slopes gently with its burden of meadows and corn fields to the water's edge; then towers into stark precipitous headlands, around whose base the thwarted waves rage and resound for ever. From misty chasms in the hills, the cloudlike woodlands dip their branches into the waves; and in many a dark cavern the green waves sob in eternal monotone.'

Later, Neville Shute in *The Lonely Road*, sailing into Torquay harbour, waxed lyrical over the magical town, with white walls and gleaming gold and blue towers shining iridescently in

Scene across the harbour from Princess Pier

The Imperial's impressive location

Torquay's Age of Elegance. This extremely early photograph, taken in the 1860s, looks out over the growing town. The majority of the elegant villas dotting the hillsides would all have been built within a few years of this photo being taken.

the morning light. Paul Gogarty in *The Coast Road* is in a similar eulogizing vein as he takes in the panorama from his Imperial balcony, slowly sinking with the sun into a pantheistic, pinot-grigio-fuelled, nirvana.

You do have to admit, however, that what you are seeing takes some beating. Torbay is a spectacular arc of coast by any standards. And yet in the resort stakes, Torquay was slow off the mark, lagging behind neighbours like Teignmouth and Dawlish. The town got officially 'discovered' towards the end of the eighteenth century, around 1789 to be precise, when the French Revolution put the Cannes and Nice Riviera off-limits and George III launched the fad for sea-water bathing.

At that time, of course, Torquay was a winter resort. The Imperial advertised lower prices in the off-peak summer season as it was considered far too hot for one's health during the months of July and August. The town is sheltered by its hills from the piercing winds of the north, east and west, the seas are warmed by the effects of the Gulf Stream, and therefore the bay enjoys its own micro-climate which enables semi-exotics – palms, vines and the like – to flourish. Due to such an equable set of affairs, it was considered particularly suitable for those suffering from consumption and similar ailments.

There were two ways of looking at this. *Harper's New Monthly Magazine* describes it thus: 'The beach was crowded with people, for it was early morning and fine weather, and all Torquay was abroad. Some were sauntering on the beach, others on the terraces, and several invalids were being slowly drawn up and down in bath chairs in the white streak of sunlight that divided the rocky beach from the first terrace, and it was hard to bear in mind that this was actual wintertime, and in England.'

An American visitor to the bay had a slightly different take on the matter: 'Torquay, I have said, has an unusual amount of wealthy people. It has also a seeming monopoly of invalids. Some days, I found the pleasure of our walks along Rock Walk and the sands perfectly destroyed by the number of infirm old people, and still more lamentable, deathly looking young people who haunt that particular place of pleasure. I have almost concluded that a too famous health resort cannot be a healthy place…'[1]

History proved our American guest wrong. The arrival of the railway in 1848 gave a further boost to the resort. There were one or two modest hotels and lodging houses, but at its beginnings, the fashion was to rent out entire villas for the season. This continued on into the early 1900s. The Millers, in fact, would rent out Ashfield, in this manner, on several occasions.

However, in the 1860s Sir Lawrence Palk, chairing the newly-formed Torquay Hotel Company, decided that the time was ripe for a modern hotel to rival the best in Europe and really put Torquay on the world map. As for the location, the company would purchase the leases of two villas to the east of the harbour named The Cove and The Cliff. The project was greatly aided by the fact that Sir Lawrence was owner of all the land to the east of the harbour.

Early postcards show the hotel as a rather oversized, top-heavy villa perching on the edge of the cliff. Not that that worried the proprietors. In the *Torquay Times* of 3 November 1866, they were proud to vaunt 'The colossal structure, designated most appropriately the Imperial Hotel, is now open for the reception of the *distingué*.' A sumptuous banquet *a la Russe* was organized for directors and friends.

No expense had been spared on the interior. The brochure talks of decorated zinc verandahs and shades, Spanish mahogany fittings, Sienna marble pilasters, Brazilian marble mantelpieces and lavatories supplied with hot and cold water. There was also an elaborate system of bells so that guests could summon their domestics when required.

It was an instant success. Within two years, additional wings were already being considered. Royal patronage came swiftly, too. The Queen of the Netherlands arrived with her considerable entourage. Napoleon III dropped in for health reasons. The visitor's book features magnificent names like Prince Esterhazy of Pesth and

(Top) The Imperial Hotel perched on the edge of the cliff

(Bottom) The walk from the Imperial to Meadfoot

Adalbert, Prince of Prussia. Then there are also your real A-listers such as The Prince of Wales, the future King Edward, who was drawn to the bay for a variety of reasons – mostly female.

The hotel was still very much in vogue in the 1930s, and could count amongst its guests, Princess Beatrice, the ex-king Alfonso of Spain – and a certain Hercule Poirot (The Imperial appears in three novels. The Grand never got a look in).

Poirot was the first of Agatha's detectives to visit the hotel, together with his sidekick, Hastings, in *Peril at End House* in 1932. Torquay is St Loo. The Imperial is the Majestic. Hastings regards the town as the jewel of the English Riviera deserving its reputation as the Queen of Watering Places. Typically, Agatha cannot resist placing it on the Cornish Coast.

The novel starts on the terrace of the hotel. Poirot and Hastings are admiring the sub-tropical gardens, guests are basking in the sun on an unusually warm August day. Sea and sky are the same deep blue.

The perfect setting for a murder. Or rather, an attempt at murder, which would have gone unnoticed, had it not been for Poirot's legendary powers of observation.

The intended victim lives at End House, a villa up a sharp hill to the right of the hotel. We learn from Poirot's visit that the house is large, stands near the edge of the cliff, is shut in by trees and in urgent need of repair

The real-life inspiration of End House was Rock End. It originally stood on the promontory past the hotel. The imposing house would have looked down today on to the Imperial's swimming pool. The original building has long gone, swallowed up by the tentacular development that now grips the headland.

It was built by Richard Harvey (owner of Greenway) around 1840. With 6 best bedrooms, 3 dressing rooms and 9 servant rooms it stood in a park of 20 acres.

Although the house is no more, it is still possible to gain a good idea of its incredible location. Leave the car-park above the Osborne Hotel and turn left up the hill. You soon pass Villa Syracusa as the path curves round to the right. Once on Daddyhole Plain make towards the far corner. The arch marks the entrance to Rock End land. The views back to Thatcher rock are spectacular. The pathway skirts the outer wall of the original property, passing at one point under a tower used as a lookout. In 1940 our valiant Home Guard were stationed here with rocks and boulders ready to repel the anticipated Nazi invasion.

Initially it's quite a tame walk, with great views out over the bay. However, just past the watch tower, the path has a gung-ho moment and suddenly takes a precipitous descent 100 metres down the cliff face, with stunning views to the sea below.

(Right) The Imperial, with Rock End to the right amongst the trees

View from the Imperial's terrace

THE IMPERIAL HOTEL

Thatcher Rock from Daddyhole Plain

In 1942, it was the turn of Miss Marple to visit the hotel. In *The Body in the Library* Colonel Bantry finds a platinum blonde, white-diamante-clad young woman on the floor of his library. The victim is one Ruby Keene, 18, a professional dance-hostess at the Majestic Hotel, Danemouth. One of the hotel staff upon whom suspicion falls is Raymond Starr, a tall, deeply tanned hunk of a professional tennis and dancing coach.

(Left) Rock End watch tower

(Right) The natural arch known as 'London Bridge'

Strangely enough, about the only aspect of the hotel that Agatha chooses to describe are the rather dingy rooms set aside for staff and the occasional guest when the hotel is crammed to the eaves. The rooms, we are told, are furnished with the oak and mahogany wardrobes stripped out of the old-style luxury suites when the hotel was modernised.

In 1976 the hotel takes its swansong as itself, in the denouement of *Sleeping Murder*. Agatha, ever the joker, sets the novel in Dillmouth, which to all intents and purposes describes Torquay. That is, until just before the end when the scene shifts to the Imperial – in Torquay. The ever-sprightly Miss Marple, Gwenda and Giles sit on the terrace and the (very) elderly detective explains how things had gone. The closing lines of the novel have Miss Marple smiling, looking out over Torbay.

Towards the end of the 1950s, like an adversary of the mafia who ends up on the losing side, the elegant Imperial gets itself encased in concrete and comes to assume the appearance it has today. The original hall and some of the original interior remain, such as the staircase and the bar to the left which leads out on to the terrace.

I suppose large, white, rectangular blocks were the fashion, the shape of things to come, at that time. And, in fairness, it must be said that we are by no means the first to complain that the town has been spoilt by new development. Russell in his *History of Torquay* tells us that a certain W S Landor lamented as far back as 1837 that 'since he first saw Torquay forty years previously, six or seven thatched cottages had been replaced by smart, ugly houses and rich, hot-looking people'.

The 1950s, and especially the 60s, in Torquay did see, however, some spectacularly dodgy planning decisions going through. Some of the more 'outstanding' examples still dominate the harbour. I refer, of course, to the Shirley Towers (locally known as the Three Ugly Sisters), and adjacent developments on Vane and Walden Hill.

It was not only what they looked like, but where they put them, that jars. One starts to hatch the suspicion that developers, builders, councillors and planners all inhabited the secluded villas far above the town, out of sight of the eyesores that they were creating. Professor

The Shirley towers – the Three Ugly Sisters

Pevsner's palette of epithets used to paint the scene wrought by the 1960s on the Torquay skyline ranges from 'callous' and 'disastrous', through 'inept' and 'ludicrous', to 'undistinguished' and 'ungainly'.

Not that, at the time, there weren't objectors. Back in 1960, a petition was presented to the Torquay Planning committee concerning the construction of four blocks totalling 172 flats in the Warberries. The protest letter stated that the proposed buildings would: (i). be unsightly and visible over a very wide area; (ii). effect the amenities of the surrounding neighbourhood and (iii). be inappropriate and entirely out-of-keeping with the character of the immediate neighbourhood, and would dominate Torquay's lovely coastline and picturesque hills. The Council's decision? 'The committee considered the petition and confirmed its recommendation of the application'.

The 'Pagoda' (top right) on Waldon Hill

Having said all that, it is Agatha in her autobiography who tells us (thinking back to her mother who used to fall asleep reading to her, and whose glasses would then fall off her nose leaving her looking slightly ridiculous) that when we love someone, we love them in spite of, maybe even because of, their imperfections.

What I mean is that now, after so long (and I almost believe this), it's difficult to imagine Torquay without its 'landmarks' of the Shirley Towers, the 'Pagoda' and the Imperial.

It just wouldn't be Torquay, I suppose.

NOTES

[1] She goes on to say that 'I have seen more luxury since being in Torquay than in all my previous life, and I know I never saw such pitiable poverty before. Half-clad childen with hungry pinched faces, and grown up beggars with something worse than either hunger or squalour upon their countenance are to be seen everywhere.'

The Victorians were an odd Jekyll and Hyde-like bunch. (Not that we seem to be much different for that matter). I have done research into my own family tree and discovered the abominable, inhumane, living conditions of the workers in the Ancoates cotton mill areas of Manchester in the first half of the 1800s, especially for Irish immigrants. In addition, although the Victorians fought for the abolishment of slavery, they could easily turn a blind eye to the fair-trade provenance or otherwise of the cotton being used in their mills. In America in 1800 there were 1 million slaves. Due in great part to the number being used in the Mississippi cotton fields that number had increased to 4.5 million by 1860. Similarly, the same census in Torquay could show a gentleman, wife and five children in a grand villa in the Warberries with 13 servants ranging from Governess to coachman, whereas a two-up, two-down near the site of the old hospital housed five families – a total of 21 people. It would seem that the upper classes, given the fact that they provided board and lodgings for so many in service, felt their consciences eased and so could forget the rest of the population slaving in mines and factories. There was upstairs, downstairs, and the rest.

16
CHURSTON STATION

The ABC Murders, Dead Man's Folly

Agatha Christie loved trains. They are right up there on her list of favourites, along with sunshine, apples and crossword puzzles.

Little wonder then that they feature so frequently in her writings. There is *Murder on the Orient Express*, and *4.50 from Paddington,* and on every other page in her autobiography she seems to be either getting on or off a train. She says somewhere, lamenting the modern train, that it is such a pity that one no longer has engines that seem to be personal friends.

Not, that is, that she always had the smoothest of journeys. Her trips on the Orient Express were routinely plagued by bedbugs which made her quite ill on more than one occasion.

Today I have come to Paignton Station on the Paignton & Dartmouth Steam Railway to take a trip back in time. For someone of my age a trip on a steam train is a journey straight back into childhood.

Even before we start I'm there with the enthusiasts, snapping the locomotives, watching the driver fill the boiler. How many hours did I spend in my youth standing on empty platforms crossing off numbers in my spotter's book? Forty years ago I would have had the courage to ask to get up on the footplate. Now I just content myself with a glimpse of the roaring fire from the platform.

The step up into the carriage reveals that this Pullman car was built in 1921 in Lincoln. It reminds me of Christie's account of Max Mallowan's preference for Pullman cars in a passage at the beginning of *Come tell Me How You Live*. It's a book in which she shows her

(Above) *Preparations for departure*

(Right) *The Pullman car*

detractors her wonderful ability to quickly and deftly sketch character, reminiscent of the travel writings of Evelyn Waugh. The first chapter tells of the preparations, the buying of clothes, the packing, and the subsequent departure from Victoria Station on a trip – once again on that Orient Express – to an archaeological dig in Iraq.

The carriages were so much more private than nowadays. There are compartments and booths rather than the impersonal open-plan layouts of modern trains. Doors curiously have changed very little – England is still about the only country in the world where to make your exit from the train you have to pull down the window, lean out precariously and joggle with the handle. The seats have that spongy, old, velvety mattress feel with the occasional rogue spring to contend with. Memories come flooding back.

The guard passes flag in hand. A whistle from him, a wave of the flag, a whistle from the locomotive and we are OFF.

The convoy creaks and clanks into life. You feel the repeated tugs as the engine takes up the strain. Nothing can take you more quickly back in time to the Christie era. The clouds of smoke pass the windows and the smell of soot fills the air. The train builds up momentum and the familiar, reassuring chuff-chuff takes over. We go over a level-crossing – strange how people always feel compelled to wave at a passing steam train.

The railway came to Paignton in 1859. The station initially stood in the middle of marshes and only a rough road constructed by the GWR lead back to the centre of town. An arrival on the late train must have been an eerie experience back then.

The line was closed down but rescued immediately by the Dart Valley Railway Company in 1973. Our locomotive today (for the train buffs) is Goliath – a 5205 class 2-8-0T tank engine, number 5239, built in 1924 and used to pull coal trains in South Wales until 1963.

We make a brief stop at Goodrington Halt before continuing on to Churston Ferrers which was originally the station for the fish market in Brixham. Hardy holidaymakers on the red sandy

(Left) Goliath

(Right) Goliath at Kingswear

(Left) The approach to Churston Station

(Right) Entering Churston Station

Flowers on the platform

beach are trying valiantly, beneath leaden skies, to make the most of the temporary respite in the torrential rain. It has been the worst August since records began. Despite the ever-more-present threat of global warming, temperatures are barely out of the fifties. The old-fashioned windbreak seems to have given way to bivouac type tents which wouldn't be out of place on an arctic expedition. Still, given today's conditions these are probably extremely practical.

Next comes the Broadsands viaduct: built, or at least inspired, by Brunel, it gives a spectacular view across the bay and also way down into perfectly tended gardens.

I open the window and stick my head out for the arrival into Churston, and instantly remember what smoke feels like when it gets in your eyes.

This is the exact same journey, the same stop – Nassecombe Station – that Hercule Poirot makes in *Dead Man's Folly*. Alighting here, he surrenders his ticket and boards the waiting Humber saloon that will take him to his meeting with Ariadne Oliver at Nasse House (Greenway).

This is also Hercule's destination in the *ABC Murders* as he arrives to investigate the murder of Carmichael Clarke. In this novel Churston plays itself. Poirot takes the midnight train from Paddington, a train Agatha Christie was very familiar with herself, to travel on the Great Western Railway the 200 and three quarter miles to the village of Churston. This was Agatha's local station when in residence at Greenway and she was a regular but, by all accounts, as befits her character, an extremely unobtrusive and unassuming passenger on her frequent trips to publishers in the capital.

CHURSTON STATION

Another train pulls up at the opposite platform on its way back to Paignton. As we move away carriages slip past each other and there is a momentary glimpse into other lives in opposite compartments. The key incident of *4.50 from Paddington* – a murder seen between trains – springs to mind and one realises how the themes for her novels grew so often out of her everyday experiences.

The track slopes gently down to the Greenway tunnel which takes the railway beneath the Greenway estate. A predecessor of Agatha's at Greenway, Richard Harvey, had not shared Mrs Christies' passion for trains and vigorously opposed the Paignton to Dartmouth line.

And then we emerge, and the ground falls away to the Dart on the right. Ancient oak woods flank the track. We pass Noss boatyard and are soon running alongside the river. We can see the higher ferry, its paddle wheels pulling it across the river. The rather austere red-brick Dartmouth Royal Naval College looks down over the town from high on the hill. Training ground for various royals over the years, this is – I may as well tell you, if not, someone else will – where the very young Princess Elizabeth first set her eyes on the equally young naval cadet Phillip.

The Station, Dartmouth. This was built before Richard Harvey's successful campaign to divert the line under Greenway to Kingswear.

(Above) Goodbye!

(Right) The Steam Packet Inn, Kingswear

We arrive at our destination, Kingswear station, which, along with the Steam Packet Inn, featured in the film 'The French Lieutenant's Woman' with Meryl Streep.

There is just time, before Goliath chugs back up the track, to join the crowd of steam groupies assembled round the locomotive for a last photo of what has become, even on this briefest of journeys, almost a friend.

17
ELBURY COVE

The ABC Murders

It's early evening in August. The occasional jogger and dog-walker pass by as the sun is setting. The persistent, plaintiff 'kiew-kiew' that I've heard since I got out of the car, suddenly reveals itself from the thick woods to the right when a (not-so-little) little owl, brown-grey fringed with white, swoops low across the fields only to disappear just as quickly into towering trees further along the golf course. The air is warm. Two men in a boat are pulling in crab-pots off towards Brixham. There are brambles and bracken. This is the place.

The paths around Elbury Cove are the setting for the key incident in the Hercule Poirot story, *The ABC Murders*. It is here that Sir Carmichael Clarke, unfortunately for him, has his head stove in with a blunt instrument whilst enjoying his evening constitutional.

Little has changed on the path since the 1930s when Clarke met his demise. There are three main ways of approaching this delightful beach: down through the woods on the southern side after crossing Churston links, by skirting the headland from Broadsands, or by taking the

(Left) A summer evening at Elbury

(Right) Shadows lengthen on the beach

Dawn over Torquay

(Left) Dawn and dew, Elbury

(Right) Sunrise over the bay

diagonal path in front of the bungalows (you can park in Brunel Road and take a cut through the houses), over the stile, and taking a right at the fork. It's this last way which best corresponds to the description of the path Inspector Crome takes with Franklin Clarke, the victim's brother, down to the sea on their way to view the scene of the crime.

It's here, at Elbury, that this book really first came into being. Years ago when I taught English in Italy I used to do a 'superlative' lesson along the lines of, 'What's the most beautiful place you ever visited?', 'What's the most important thing you ever forgot?' A typical old chestnut of an EFL lesson. Anyway, as a warmer, I used to do a quiz where the students had to guess the locations of breathtaking landscapes that I showed them. There were ten or so – some classics –the Maldives, Namibia, the Alps, then one or two trickier ones, and then the last was always a photo of Elbury Cove. And what a stunner of a photo it was – dark green woods cascading down to the sea; deep, deep blue water; a yacht moored a few metres off a beach of dazzling white.

I got lots of wrong answers for that last question – the Seychelles, the Croatian coast, somewhere in the Mediterranean. And then I could proudly reveal that this was where I came from – Devon, Torbay, Elbury Cove – my favourite beach since I had been a child. And what's more – what a coincidence (well, I had to earn a living), I was organising a study-holiday there the following summer at my father's language school.

Much, much later, writing an article to promote Devon in a language travel magazine, I came across the paragraph describing Elbury in *The ABC Murders* and found Agatha Christie shared my opinion exactly. Clarke and Crome reach a ridge overlooking the cove and Clarke (unusually in an Agatha Christie novel) waxes lyrical over the beauty of the place.

So, when I decided to embark on this project, this was the obvious place to start.

It's a wonderful spot to come in the morning, at sunrise, too. Not that you are alone. Depending on the route you take, well before 7.00am there are dog-walkers and even people bathing in the sea.

The path via the headland affords magnificent views across the bay and craggy headlands beyond, jutting out into the sea. If you sit at this time of the morning, all you can hear is the mill-pond calm sea lapping against the hollows of the rock beneath you. The water is perfectly

transparent, the sun's rays are fanned through the clouds like a painting by William Blake. Across the hazy morning air, on the other side of the cove, an enigmatic ruin stands with its feet in the clear, chilled water.

OK, once you actually get down on the beach, it's a bit more prosaic. The glistening white is in fact large whitish-pinkish pebbles. These are incredibly painful to walk on barefoot and phenomenally uncomfortable for sunbathing (the best place is, in fact, the flat rocks on the left of the cove).

However as a youngster, as I was saying, it was my favourite beach – perhaps because it was a bit of a secret amongst the locals. And although it is years now since I have swum regularly in England (once you get used to the Mediterranean, it is difficult to go back to our near-zero temperatures), this was the place even I came to for a dip that famous August day the other year when the thermometer hit 38 at Heathrow and most of the country started to melt.

The beach was formerly the private property of Lord Churston and at the far end of the cove can still be seen the nineteenth century sea-water bathing house that he had built there for Lady Churston. Originally thatched, it housed two large copper cylinders filled with sea water, one of which was heated, enabling my lady to pass from a steaming hot tub in the first to an exhilarating cold dip in the second (there is more about this regally-driven health fad in the earlier chapter on Greenway).

Returning to *The ABC Murders*, chapter 15 finds Agatha, unusually, filling us in on the location – Churston – for the Carmichael murder. We even get some comments on the local

(Left) Lord Churston's bathing house. An early photograph taken when it was still in use

(Right) The bathing house glimpsed across the cove

Looking down on to the cove

The Bathing House, 1937 (The ABC Murders was published in 1936)

urban planning situation. In the past the arc between Brixham and Paignton had been an unspoilt stretch of countryside whereas now new houses had started to dot the coastline. Carmichael's own house is described as a white rectangle of modern design which was 'not unpleasing to the eye'.

A bit of research reveals that a proposed housing development in this area was, in fact, quite an issue amongst the locals at the time. Dartington Hall with its ground-breaking ideas for society had, through its building division, Staverton Builders, commissioned a high profile Swiss-American architect, William Lescaze, best known for his PSFS tower in Philadelphia, to design a housing complex for Churston in the International Modernist style. Lescaze had recently built a house – High Cross – for the headmaster at Dartington School and the Elmhirsts, (the couple who inspired the Dartington project) had high hopes for a development along these lines. The houses were to be sited along the road down to Broadsands. There was even to be a hotel on the headland. The houses were, as Christie says, modern, all white, functional, horizontals and verticals with flat roofs and broad expanses of glass and concrete.

In 1933 the *Totnes Times* and *Devon News* attacked the project not only for spoiling an intact bathing region but also, somewhat parochially, because Americans were involved. To further aggravate matters, the houses were significantly more expensive than other houses being

Lescaze House

produced at the time by competitors. Opposition grew. To support the ailing project, Lescaze, himself, was brought over at the end of 1934 to give a presentation entitled 'Why we have adopted Modern Architecture'.

However, despite these efforts and the production of a brochure to sell more houses, which Christie herself would certainly have read, only six houses had been sold by the beginning of 1935 and the major investor in the hotel project had pulled out.

You can see the brochure in the archive at Highcross House. It is a beautiful object in its own right, illustrated with superb watercolours. It does, however, shoot itself in the foot. It begins by extolling this part of the coast as one of the last unspoilt stretches of coastline left in the country, but finishes with a map which shows how the development would stretch all down the valley and cover the headland with a hotel on the most prominent point.

Eventually, Dartington gave up on the idea and De Soissons, the architect of Welwyn Garden City fame, was brought in to design more traditional pitched-roof houses (examples in Tor Close) and produce a revised plan for the estate.

The six or so original houses Lescaze designed are still there overlooking the viaduct – and marvellous houses they are too. In Torquay, on the hills above Livermead, there other examples of this modernist style of architecture. The best examples of inter-war architecture in Torquay town centre are of the same school.

Quite how the British manage to be so conservative in their appreciation of house design is hard to fathom. As it was then, it's the same today – nothing has changed in 70 years – just look at the new estates going up all around.

Agatha Christie appears to have had a foot in both camps. She obviously appreciated the clean lines of the Lescaze houses – she spent a lot of time removing Victorian add-ons from Greenway, restoring it to its geometrically pure Georgian form. But you also feel she would have been against the development of what was clearly one of her favourite places to swim.

And, you know what... sitting here on my headland at quarter to seven watching the sun come up, I am sure even I would have spoken out against the hotel!

18

THE PRINCESS GARDENS

The ABC Murders

(Opposite page) The Princess Gardens and the Pavilion from Vane Hill

The Gardens looking towards the Pavilion

The Princess Gardens were opened in 1894. These were the new, have-you-seen-them-yet gardens where Agatha Christie would have come as a child.

Originally, the area where the pavilion stands now was a beach which doubled as a building refuse dump. This is where the Flete Brook (which used to run down present Fleet street) emptied into the sea. It was tidied up and made into Cary Green. At first it vaunted a cannon used at Sebastopol as a victory trophy. Very quickly it was decided that the trophy was likely to cause offence to visiting Russian royal family members in the town and it was moved.

When the plans for the new Princess Pier were approved it was decided to widen the road under the present Rock Walk and reclaim from the sea three acres of land between the Pavilion and the Princess Pier. 200 000 tons of material were needed to complete the operation.

A *Wellingtonia gigantica* was planted to mark the occasion – the Victorians loved everything to do with the famous General. Quite how the local officials imagined that such a monster – they can grow to 50 metres and weigh up to 2460 tons – would fit in with the surroundings is a mystery. They were certainly going for duration: specimens regularly live between 1500 and 3000 years. It was the mayor who had the honour of shovelling in the earth around its roots. His fingers were clearly far from green: it died prematurely just a few weeks later.

Torbay Council, ever alert to the possibility of making a swift buck, initially installed paying turnstiles to allow strollers to enter the park for twopence. Naturally, an uproar ensued and the turnstiles were promptly removed. Images of the time show elegant couples taking refreshments at the tables of the waterside cafes. There are bandstands and steamers, and J Class yachts in the new harbour enclosed by the recent Princess Pier. The owner of the Torbay Hotel, Mr Young, presented the Council with the marvellous fountain at a cost of £150. Flowerbeds were planted with the patriotic reds, whites and blues of geranium, marguerite and lobelia. The whole effect was completed with fairy lamps – little lanterns with real candles! For the first time, Torbay Council launched a nationwide advertising campaign to present the resort to the nation.

(Left) Mr Young's ornamental fountain

(Centre) The fountain with the Pavilion behind

(Right) The fountain – a blue study

Today, Torquay continues with its advertising campaigns. The target market, it must be said, has changed somewhat since then. The resort has become a prime destination for pre-nuptial binge weekends and, rather than aristocratic-looking blazered flaneurs on the prom, you are far more likely to come across herds of Elvis lookalikes, or red-wigged rock-chicks making their way from hotels and bed & breakfasts to their high-octane stag and hen appointments.

Agatha Christie would remember the park when she came to write *The ABC Murders*. Mr Cust, one of the chief suspects, would emerge from the Torquay Pavilion (it doubled as a picture house), sit in one of the shelters facing Torquay harbour, and read with trembling hands in the local paper of the murder of Sir Carmichael Clarke at Churston. The shelters (not the originals),

The original café in the Gardens

A dolphin in sunlight

THE PRINCESS GARDENS

(Left) Showing at the Princess Theatre this week…

(Right) Fountain with the War Memorial behind

are still there. What I personally like best is Mr Young's fountain (there is a similar one in the Raffles Hotel in Singapore), with sunlight playing on the dolphins and the water babies, the flower beds and the Torbay palms.

White, in his *History of Torquay* remembers how the Princess Theatre project was pushed through at the end of the 1950s and laments the lack of 'vocal opposition' on the part of the residents. Recently there has been talk again of 'developing' (i.e. building over) the Gardens. This would mean losing another of the main natural attractions of the bay.

19
BURGH ISLAND

And Then There Were None, Evil Under the Sun

There is something about islands. Surrounded by water, cut off, stranded – but with a terrific opportunity for adventure: *Robinson Crusoe, Swallows and Amazons, Swiss Family Robinson* – magical reads from my childhood.

Add another layer: the island in question sports an art deco hotel which has hosted the likes of Noel Coward, Winston Churchill, King Edward VIII and Mrs Simpson. The icing on the cake for Agatha Christie fans: it's the setting for one of the best known whodunits of all time: *And Then There Were None*. The cherry on the top: perhaps the most famous of all the island's guests – Hercule Poirot in *Evil under the Sun*.

Driving through the narrow lanes you get snatched glimpses of the sea, then finally the road drops down and the island is there in front of you – its hotel gleaming white in the morning sun. 'It lives up to expectation,' to quote a character from *And Then There Were None*.

The first glimpse of Burgh Island

Parking up and going down to the beach I am faced with the predicament of how to get across to the island. It's before 8am, there is no-one around. But I'm in luck – there is a Range Rover coming down the slipway on the island and loading luggage on the strange contraption at the bottom of the ramp. Minutes later, the sea tractor – a platform on stilts driven by enormous wheels with tread six inches deep – is ploughing through the waves towards the mainland. As we trundle back across, the sun is still coming up through the mist over Bantham.

The Hotel from the mainland

(Top) The sea tractor

(Bottom) Looking back towards Bantham

(Left) Teeth-like rocks

(Centre) Evening primrose covers the island

(Right) The coast from the island

I am the first of the non-hotel visitors today. I move off, passing the Pilchard Inn. A sign tells me that the top bar is exclusively for the use of hotel residents. The hotel has a sign too indicating that beyond this point only guests may venture. You don't feel completely welcome – in the past owners have tried to bar the public completely from the island – they haven't succeeded, the public footpaths have been here for too long.

The first cove I come to has wonderfully transparent, blue-green water and menacing, black, jagged, teeth-like rocks protecting its privacy.[1]

A sign of the times

The Pilchard Inn sign

Climbing the hill there are yellow and pink flowers everywhere. Reaching the top, and busy congratulating myself that I am only semi-out-of-breath, I find to my horror that I am unknowingly standing within inches of a giddy-making, sheer drop of hundreds of feet. I don't like heights – my hands are tingling and sweating just remembering it – I would have been glad of some sort of warning. I notice that slightly further around this yawning chasm is a sign – facing the other way. Upon inspection it reads 'dang rous clif s'.

The ruined building was apparently originally a chapel (they still bless wind-swept married couples up here) and then went on to become the Huer's hut from which the look-out would cry to launch the boats as soon as he has spied a shoal of pilchards.

I know from Tony Porter's book *The Great White Palace* that there is still a metal ladder leading down the cliff to one of the coves, a ladder which played such an important part in *Evil under the Sun*. This fact I will have to take on trust – there is no way I am going to check it out.

Skirting the hotel grounds, I decide to drop in and grab a brochure. The girl at the reception is most pleasant but makes it clear I cannot take a peek at the famous mermaid pool that features so prominently in the same novel.

Back outside the Pilchard Inn I realize to my chagrin that it is still too early to research this aspect of the island. The tide is just turning and there is a narrow strip visible back to the mainland. Dispelling my fears of quicksand – I have read somewhere that more than one US jeep came to grief and is buried here – I step confidently out. Underfoot, however, is remarkably firm. A barefoot waitress passes me going the other way.

(Left) The Pilchard Inn

(Right) The walk to work

Back in the car-park I have a glance at the hotel brochure. It's not cheap. But then a place which has such an illustrious visitor's book is hardly likely to be.

Almost a year later and an important birthday coming up. Why not celebrate with a night on the island? Although I ring a good two months in advance, the hotel is so booked up that the first available room is two week's after the historic milestone. The island, apparently, is popular for marriages; for a mere ten grand or so you can book the whole works (for a night) for you and your guests.

No matter - we book ourselves in. The Mermaid Suite sounds enchanting – southerly sea views over the mermaid pool. A glamorous bedroom with one of their larger double beds. Bedroom furniture is 'Queenie's', one of the hotel's regular party-loving guests. Perfect!

The next day a letter arrives in the post. It indicates what time we should arrive to coincide with low-tide. Otherwise, if weather conditions are bad the proprietors cannot guarantee access to the island by the sea tractor.

There's more: 'Our guests dress formally for dinner; black tie and 'proper' evening dress is required'. I jot down in the diary a note to find out about hiring a DJ.

Driving down through Slapton and Kingsbridge reminds me of the opening of *And Then There Were None* when all the characters are presented to the reader as they arrive for their appointment by their various means of transport. We have also been given instructions for our arrival. We are to stop at Bigbury Golf Course and telephone the hotel to obtain the secret code for the day. It's already getting quite exciting and we haven't even got there yet. Code duly memorized (ok it was only for the carpark key-pad) we proceed on down the hill. Past the red phone box, in with the code and here we are. Extra careful not to scratch anything, we park between a Porsche and a Ferrari. Scarcely have we opened the boot than the Land Rover is here to greet us.

The room, rather the suite, is a palette of light and dark blues and grey. A Bush radio is playing softly. 'Queenie's' bedroom furniture has the most marvellous honey hues and amazing grain effects giving continually changing shapes, faces and patterns a bit like a Rorschach test.

Everything is geometric – all squares, steps and zig-zags. Rachel has already fallen in love with the curtains which I am ordered to photograph for future reference. The box of chocolates that lay in wait for us on the bed survives a couple of minutes, if that.

The Mermaid Suite

(Left) The ladder down to Pixy's cove

(Right) Pixy's cove

The view from the window is just as Poirot described it. It is out of season so the floats, lilos, balls and rubber toys have gone, but the deck chairs on the terraces leading down to the bathing beach are still there and the raft is anchored in the middle of the pool. The path leading off round the cliff to 'Sunny Ledge' (as shown on the map in the novel *Evil under the Sun*), scene of many intimate conversations between characters, is still there, too.

I get the feeling there are more coves than Agatha has shown on her map of the island and realize later that I had unknowingly photographed the top of the steel ladder leading down to Pixy Cove in one of my more courageous ventures towards the cliff edge. As for seeing the beach where Arlena Marshall's body was found, you would need a boat to do that.

Christie would have known Archie Nettlefold through his theatre connections in London. It was he who made in 1929 the building as we see it today. The 'Great White Palace' was already famed for its 'racy' parties, with flapper girls, white ladies and screwdrivers, well before it became a hotel in 1933. Christie must have visited after 1934 because she mentions right at the start of *Evil under the Sun* important modifications made to the hotel in that year.

We visit the Pilchard Inn for lunch. It's the first chance to weigh up our fellow guests – some definitely have 'the look' be it natural or studied – others less so. The fire-side bar is reserved for guests of course – how smug it feels to be on the other side this time. The barman is impressively knowledgeable – try this rosé it has a lovely taste of biscuit – and totally in, and yet out of, control at the same time. We have been in only a couple of minutes and he knows my name – your crab and spring onion baguette Mr Hawthorne. Rachel's arrives down from the 'big hoos' elaborately wrapped in fresh towels.

This is, of course, the multi-talented cocktail-king, Gary, from Fife – I have read about him – he's been a fixture on the island since 1996. His continuous babble of benevolent banter has the whole company smiling and chuckling immediately. What a difference the right staff can make.

Back in the room and flicking through the 'Welcome' folder again we read that: 'Most of our guests will be down for a snifter in the Palm Court by 7pm'. Also that we should not worry about being overdressed, 'as this is simply impossible!' Rachel tells me that this is exactly what her mother always said to her and what she now tells her own children. I have a feeling Rachel's mother would have loved this place. Just as I am starting to feel rather self-important we hear a helicopter arrive and land on the pad near the tennis court. Point taken!

The Mermaid Pool is right in front of our window. The shadows are lengthening over the rippled water. Back in the 1930s the cove was still open to the sea, allowing yachts to moor at the steps. Since then its entrance has been walled up and now it remains full even at low tide. It was on the terrace below me that Poirot, resplendent in his white duck suit and panama hat, made his comments (woefully sexist as usual), regarding the sunbathers down on the beach – comments which will prove so telling later in the book. It is also from here that early one morning he helps Arlena Marshall launch her white wooden float, soaking his white suede shoes in the process. He watches her – white bathing dress, green Chinese hat – paddle off to her destiny.

Arlena's room had two big bay windows, with a balcony, overlooking the bathing beach and the sea. I reckon, having seen the hotel now, that it must have been either the Eddystone or the Nettlefold Suite.

The Pilchard Inn – entrance to fireside bar

The Mermaid Pool at sunset

Like Poirot and the other characters in *Evil Under the Sun*, guests watch and comment on each other. It's inevitable, the hotel is not big, there is not much space on the island. There are people of many different types and backgrounds thrown together. It is the perfect mix of location and character for a Christie mystery – one wonders how many nano-seconds it took her to come up with the idea of setting a novel on the island.

At 6.30pm the hotel is totally deserted – everyone is getting ready for dinner. And so it's on with the DJ and then down, with some trepidation, for an aperitif. The folder said it was impossible to overdress – it doesn't feel like it now.

But no – we are all dressed more or less the same. It does seem slightly unfair that my partner can wear whatever dress she likes whereas I have to dress to all intents and purposes like a waiter. There are a few frantic moments when I realize that I have no idea whether my cummerbund is on the right way up or not. I receive more than one odd glance from men clearly not comfortable with my surreptitiously eyeing up the top of their trousers!

A few minutes later, oiled by a Tom Collins, I am quite at home in my new garb, feeling I could do this on a regular basis. I start to note the variations that are available to the male – the red tie with matching accessories, the patterned cummerbund, or even… the white tuxedo.

One gent comes in and the whole lounge does a double-take – he's the photographic negative of every other man in the room. With a black shirt, and white tie he looks like a cross between a mafia boss and a vicar.

Back in the conservatory for petits fours, gazing up at the marvellous peacock dome, life feels good. Outside, the sky behind the black curve of the hill has taken on the most intense shade of blue – a solitary windblown hawthorn silhouetted against it. And then one, then two, then more and more pairs of ears are bobbing along the skyline. Borough island – burrows – that was the original island name.

Time for bed – a last look out over the pool. A dazzling Orion is filling the sky before our window. Good weather tomorrow too.

The next morning I rise early – the sun is coming up.

Sunrise over Bantham

A kestrel is blown in a wide arc around the hotel. Three shags, flying in formation like fighters trying to avoid radar, speed inches above the water towards Bantham. Seagulls, effortlessly surfing the updraughts, wheel overhead.

The rabbits on the lawn, mesmerized by the impending daybreak, suddenly scuttle for cover down the little headland, caught out like floppy-eared vampires as the first rays illuminate the cliff on the far side of the pool.

Rachel calls for me to come back to bed. Forget the fauna and flora, she has been much more impressed by the creature comforts of the room. Everything – the sheets, the enormous pillows, the bathrobes, the all-enveloping towels – is crisp, heavy, whiter-than-white, with that fresh-linen smell that you only find in hotels.

Time to relax after breakfast and prepare for the real world

And then it's time to leave. Checking out I notice photos for sale and choose one of the white grand piano in the dining room to give to Rachel. Apparently inspired by the island, the atmosphere and my 007-type attire she had had a dream which managed to involve the piece of furniture in question and her red stiletto shoes. I make a mental note to myself that we must definitely come more often…

I had gone not knowing entirely what to expect. I must say that once back it takes a fair few days to get used the grey, drab world that is not the island.

Writing this, three days after our return, a DVD arrives through the post. I know this is a clever piece of marketing – but it is also very nice. There's Gary, there's the place where we sat and hey, that's our bathroom.

I feel I need to go back – just to check my theory about the Eddystone, of course.

NOTES

[1] Not surprisingly, with this sort of welcome around the area is littered with shipwrecks. The *Villa Nova*'s captain in 1879 unfortunately mistook Bolt Tail, down the coast away, for Land's End and ran smack bang right into the island.

20
DARTMOUTH, THE RIVER DART AND ROYAL CASTLE HOTEL

Dead Man's Folly, Ordeal by Innocence

Following in Inspector Bland's footsteps and taking a cruise from Brixham to Dartmouth is still one of the most popular ways of making one's acquaintance with this idyllic, little port. Bland's particular motive for boarding the pleasure boat in *Dead Man's Folly*, we shall come to presently. For now there's still time to kill before we leave.

I haven't visited Brixham for years – and that's a mistake: it's not just a day-trip destination for the tourists as I thought, it really has a lot of character, it's a real working port and is once again right up there in the English fishing industry league. The catch includes lemon sole, turbot, and plaice together with cuttlefish and scallop. I will come back.

Trawler – Brixham harbour

The Torbay Belle

A trawler is politely moved on and we descend the steps to the *Torbay Belle*. We pass the cluster of anglers who have walked the three-quarters of a mile to the end of the breakwater and make towards the towering promontory of Berry Head. The lighthouse there is the smallest but also the highest in England. With its colonies of guillemots, fulmars, kittiwakes and shags, it's a guano-coated, seabird sanctuary of national significance. As we round the headland, and leave the shelter of the bay, the swell increases, as does the pitch (or is it the yaw?) and all of a sudden a summer mist descends on the proceedings.

The sun is still up there somewhere but for the moment the coast has become a vague outline in the haze – time to see if I can walk a more or less straight line to the bar to try the local Paignton brew that our captain recommended to us as we left harbour.

Further along the coast, without our captain's commentary, you would never know that the wooded valley we

Anglers on the breakwater

(Left) The Mew Stone

Dartmouth castle

are passing hides a luxuriant cleft of semi-tropical garden leading up to the house at Coleton Fishacre, home to Rupert D'Oyly Carte, hotel magnate and son of the impresario behind the operettas of Gilbert and Sullivan.

Not much later, the jagged contours of the Mew Stone ('mew' is a seagull in Devon dialect) emerge from the mist. Hereabouts, if you are luckier than I have ever been (and it's a clear day) you might see seals, dolphins, even basking sharks.

And then just as suddenly as it arrived the mist lifts and the entrance to the Dart is before us. Two castles, Kingswear to starboard and Dartmouth to port, stand sentinel to the approach to the river. A chain used to run between the two which could be raised to stop the passage of unwanted guests. The church on the Dartmouth side is St Petrox – a spiritual lighthouse for those at sea, and nowadays a trendy location for up-market weddings.

As we come in our knowledgeable captain points out on the Kingswear side what looks like a low thatched hut on a ledge just above water level. The 'thatch' is in fact reinforced concrete and the 'hut' housed two torpedoes to be used to protect the mouth of the river during the Second World War. High above in the trees is Brookhill, the house where during the war a young, president-to-be of France was billeted as a member of the Free France Naval Squadron – a certain Francois Mitterand.

Apart from Mitterand's clandestine motor torpedo boats, the various slipways along the banks have seen the departure of many an illustrious venture – knights on the Second and Third

(Left) Torpedo base, Kingswear

(Right) St Saviours church, Dartmouth

Crusades to the Holy Land in 1147 and 1190; ships of the realm under the leadership of Sir Walter Raleigh to combat the Spanish Armada (1588), the Pilgrim Fathers set sail from Bayard's Cove in 1620, and more recently the massed craft of the Normandy D-day landings assembled here in June 1944.

The river now opens up before you and the town of Dartmouth unfurls along the bank to your left. This is the Drymouth where Arthur Calgary lodges and gets knocked down, leading to his bout of amnesia, in *Ordeal by Innocence*. It is also the Helmouth of *Dead Man's Folly*. De Sousa's launch would have been moored amongst the plethora of vessels that always fill this broad expanse of the river. It is a stirring sight – Queen Victoria, a well-known fan of all things teutonic – was so taken with it that she named it the 'The English Rhine'.

Today it seems the whole of the South West has decided to attend Dartmouth's regatta. The town is heaving with people. The river is seething with boats. Everything that possibly could be is bedecked and festooned with bunting, every alcohol outlet besieged and beleaguered. There are even custom-built deck chairs with arm rests with integrated pint holders. The embankment crowds – six deep or more – are swigging lager from their plastic sleevers. Metres in front of them the jet set are sipping chilled wine on the sun decks of their luxury motor launches. Over the loud speaker the Master of Ceremonies describes the motley procession of historic craft passing downstream, while in mid-river, sits, like an enormous queen bee surrounded by her myriad attendants, this year's guard-ship, the 4900 ton, type 23 frigate, HMS *Argyll*.

Forcing one's way ashore near the Station Restaurant one comes to the boat float with, opposite, The Royal Castle Hotel. All this central part of the town is reclaimed land. Up until

(Left) Regatta revellers

(Centre) The sail past

(Right) HMS Argyll

(Left) Dartmouth colour

(Right) Dartmouth bistro

the beginning of the nineteenth century there was a tidal dam running the length of Foss Street, the lake behind which filled with water at high tide and was then allowed to drain out at low tie, driving the wheels of the water mills. Before this, at the start of the seventeenth century, as the town began to prosper from its sea trade, the need for a decent waterfront to unload vessels lead to the area of water adjacent to St Saviours church being filled in – providing the site for the present-day hotel.

At the outset, it had been the wine trade with France which filled the town's coffers.[1] By the time the houses which would become the Royal Castle were under construction, salt cod from Newfoundland had taken over as the principal source of revenue.

In this respect, Dartmouth owes a lot to a ninth-century Pope, Nicholas I, who set out in his letter to the Bulgars his various decrees on what could and couldn't be eaten during the Catholic periods of fasting in the Church calendar. Flesh-meat (carne) was forbidden (this is the origin of *carnevale* – a valedictory party to roast beef and the like before the period of Lent). Fish, on the other hand, was perfectly acceptable during these fasts. This thumbs up for creatures with scales set a trend which would stand Dartmouth in good stead over the centuries. The town prospered magnificently from the early 1600s for more than 250 years thanks to Italy, Spain and Portugal's ever-increasing demand for fish.

You could say that Newfoundland stood at the corner of a medieval golden triangle. Ships would depart from England in the spring, laden with woollen cloth to exchange for salt in the Bay of Biscay. Salt was needed for both of the different fish-curing techniques that were adopted at the time. Portuguese, French and Spanish ships would process their catch at sea by the so-called wet bulk method – supplies of salt were poured over the layers of fresh fish in the holds and there was little need for the crew to ever step ashore.

The English, however, lacking the abundant salt supplies of their rivals, were forced to adopt a more land-based method for curing their catch, combining drying and salting. Wooden stages and drying platforms known as flakes were built on their arrival in spring. Crews would then deal with the catch ashore, turning the heavy fish, which averaged three to four kilograms, until they were properly dried, even covering them when it rained. This process, although imposed by necessity and more labour-intensive had its advantages. Cod treated like this was a far richer source of protein and thus a far more valuable and sought-after commodity on the Spanish and Portuguese markets than wet bulk or green fish.

At the end of the summer season, their holds full of cured fish, the English would set sail for the south of Europe to trade their cargo for olive oil, wine, port, dates, raisins, marmalade and other luxuries, which would then be sold on to home consumers. On top of all this, there was also trayne oil to be had – an important by-product of the above process extracted from the cod livers and used for burning in lamps. When things were going well, as they often were, the ship-owning merchants were laughing all the way to the bank.

The present-day Royal Castle Hotel is an amalgam of the houses of two such of these merchants. This charming, popular hotel built in 1639, clearly has parts which date back even earlier as the plaque on the façade of the building boasts. Thought to have been constructed using the beams of a Spanish galleon captured during the rout of the Armada (maybe the same ship that provided the forced garden labour for Humphrey Gilbert at Greenway) the two houses were fused and one of the entrances was walled up – hence the reason why the present entrance is off-centre.

Through its long history the hotel has inevitably acquired a ghost or two. Princess Mary, wife of William of Orange, who was said to have been staying at the hotel in 1688 when her husband landed in Brixham, appears apparently either inside the hotel or in a spectral carriage sent by her husband to collect her. (Quite how this was managed when the only roads into Dartmouth at that time were at best negotiable by pack-horse is not clear).

It is here, too, that we find Donald Sutherland lodging during the (totally forgettable) film version of *Ordeal by Innocence*. In the short story *The Regatta Mystery* (one of the Pollensa Bay short stories, published posthumously), the hotel, under the guise of the Royal George is the setting for a most remarkable dinner involving Mr Pointz, Mr Pyne and a disappearing diamond, which finds Agatha Christie at her most ingenious. The dinner during which the jewel miraculously vanishes is taken on the first floor at a table set in the big bulging bay window. The noise coming up from the street which causes Pointz to ask for the windows to be closed is from the fun-fair which is still held in Regatta week

And so on to Greenway (the destination on this trip for Inspector Bland), and our local hero, Sir Humphrey Gilbert, one of the estate's first residents, who, some ninety years after John Cabot, set sail to take possession of the island for his sovereign Queen Elizabeth I.

(Left) The Royal Castle Hotel

(Centre) The bay window at The Royal Castle Hotel

(Right) The lower ferry

There is a wonderful portrait in Compton Castle of a resplendent Gilbert with perfectly coiffured moustache, sporting a very natty orange tunic. It is said that Queen Elizabeth had 'a special liking' for him. However, it would appear that his sense for things sartorial far outstripped his sense for things seafaring. The Queen, no less, was even heard to remark on one occasion that he was not 'a man of good hap by sea'. He seems to have been prone, once having stepped off terra ferma, not only to extraordinarily bad luck but, more seriously, to even worse judgement.

He commenced his first voyage, sailing against the best advice of generations of fisherman before him, far too late in the season. These voyages were traditionally made, for meteorological

'Hoo Down' boathouse

considerations, only in spring or summer. He left on 23 September and immediately ran into storms, whereupon the rest of his entourage promptly deserted him. The venture was an unmitigated disaster.

Not surprisingly, it took several years to persuade anyone at all to back him on a second enterprise. Fortunately, his half-brother, Sir Walter Raleigh, put in a good word for him with Elizabeth (she had a soft spot for Raleigh, too), who eventually consented to give Gilbert her Royal patronage. She backed this up with probably one of the most expensive good luck charms of all time – a diamond-encrusted gold anchor talisman.

Unfortunately this was all to no avail. One of the ships was forced to turn back due to sickness after just a couple of days. On arrival in Newfoundland, a second ship, *The Swallow*, had to turn back as so many crew had fallen sick or died. 'Silver' was discovered which subsequently turned out to be no more than mica. Gilbert then ordered a controversial change of course for the fleet, blatantly disregarding the views of more experienced mariners in his crew. Result – *The Delight* ran aground not only with the loss of 80 hands but also with most of the stores of clothing and food for the entire expedition, as well as all the specimens of plants and ores which had been collected up to that point. Deciding to turn for home, the remaining two ships ran into atrocious weather off the Azores. Gilbert, in a rather bizarre finale, was last seen sitting astern, book in hand, quoting Thomas More's *Utopia*: 'We are as near to heaven by sea as by land'. Moments later, *The Squirrel* – a miniscule vessel of only 10 tons which – yes, you have guessed – everyone had warned was too small a craft to even be considered for such a voyage, disappeared beneath the mountainous waves.

* * * * * *

The Dart above Dittisham

Today, however, the sun is shining and our pleasure boat is more than a match for the gently-flowing Dart. As we travel on upriver, we pass the boathouses of May Pool (Hoo Down) youth hostel and Greenway (Nasse House) which featured prominently in *Dead Man's Folly*.

The loudspeakers of our Riverlink cruiser crackle into action, directing our attention to the craggy rock jutting up mid-stream – the Anchor, or Scold Stone. This is the moment Inspector Bland has been waiting for. A 1950s re-enactment à la *Crimewatch* follows which goes unnoticed by all except our champion of law and order. All this to demonstrate how it could have been done. The modus operandi of a murder has been tested and proved to have been possible. Suitably self-satisfied, the Inspector adjourns to Gitcham (Dittisham) where he smugly consumes a lobster tea complete with Devonshire clotted cream and scones.

NOTES
[1] Chaucer's *Canterbury Tales* feature a character - the Sailor – who was involved in these dealings with Bordeaux. 'A shipman was ther, wonynge fer by weste; For aught I woot, he was of dertemouthe' This merchant was most probably based on a real Dartmouth personage of the time – John Hawley. The most popular vessel used for this commerce was the cog, the same type of ship that had carried the knights out to the holy land on the Crusades. The ship depicted on the town's coat of arms transporting an enormous torso of King Edward III is a cog.

21
DITTISHAM AND GALMPTON

Dead Man's Folly, Ordeal by Innocence

The Paignton to Brixham road runs along the crest of the ridge separating Torbay, on the one side, from the River Dart on the other. At the junction known as Windy Corner, it branches off to the right and drops down into the village of Galmpton. Following the signs for Greenway, one passes in front of the village school. A plaque on the wall of Vale Cottage opposite reveals that it was here that Robert Graves, poet and novelist, resided during the Second World War. Best known for his trilogy, *I, Claudius*, Graves would have worked here on one of my personal favourites, the semi-historical novel *King Jesus*, published in 1946.

Graves, was by all accounts, a good friend of Agatha Christie, or Mrs Mallowan as she preferred to be known in the village. Curiously, they both were of the opinion, as reported in the autobiography, that the activity of washing up was one of the greatest aids to literary production – freeing the mind to soar to higher levels. A disturbing thought crosses one's mind: had the dishwasher existed back then, the two might never have risen to prominence! Christie held Graves in such esteem that she dedicated to him, in a most deferential, humble and playful tone, her novel *Towards Zero*.

Weaving one's way through the assembled four-by-fours and top-of-the-range Mercedes on the morning school run, one cannot help but muse that Galmpton, like some of its neighbours, is becoming distinctly upwardly mobile. A call to a local estate agent confirms my suspicion that a young Galmptonian would find it hard to get a digit, let alone a foot, on today's property ladder. To be fair, this first impression is tempered by a glance at the village website, which indicates that the 'Protect Village Life' committee is alive, kicking and successfully fighting to preserve its customs, ethos and traditions. Incontrovertible proof – the annual Gooseberry Pie Fair, reinstated in 1951, is not only thriving but going from strength to strength.

All this would certainly have pleased Mrs Mallowan, who took great pride in setting and judging the school's yearly essay competition (of her own inauguration) and who regularly swept the board at the Brixham horticultural and flower show. When she took over Greenway with her husband they became the latest in a long line of Lords and Ladies of the manor of

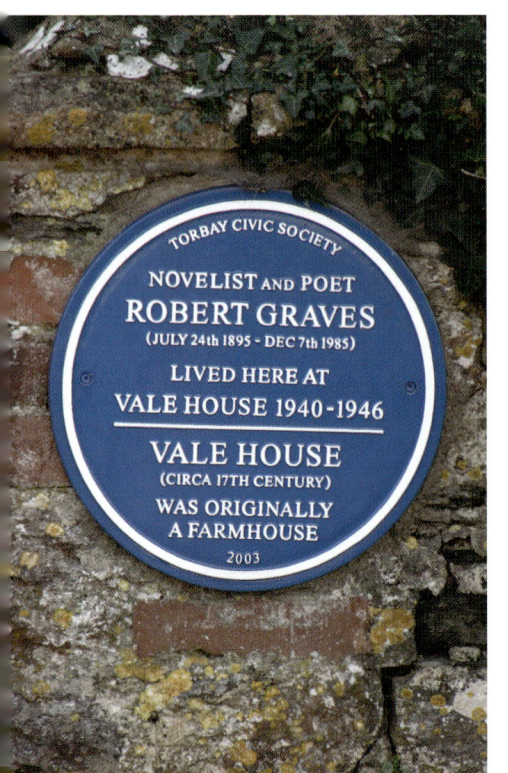

Plaque outside Robert Graves' house, Galmpton

Galmpton. Her predecessors, too, had taken an active interest in the village – the cottages opposite the school were built by Richard Harvey, as the escutcheon on the wall bears witness, to improve the standard of life in the village.

From here the car crosses the bridge over the Paignton to Kingswear steam railway line which is soon skirting the road to the left through sparse woodland. As the line again crosses under the road to disappear into the Greenway tunnel, a stunning vista of the Dart opens up to your right (Broad Reach and Galmpton Creek to be exact – the widest meander on the river at over a mile across) with, in the distance, on a clear day, Dartmoor. This is the magnificent view of the River Helm that Hercule Poirot is called upon to begrudgingly admire as he is chauffeured to Nasse House from Churston Station at the beginning of *Dead Man's Folly*.

It is also just about at this point in the journey that Poirot's car comes upon the girl hikers on their way to Hoo Down Park Hostel (today, Maypool Hostel – you will see the signposted road fork off to the left). His rather scathing comments on the combination of the female posterior and shorts have always seemed to me somewhat lacking in sincerity given that he almost immediately takes the decision to stop and give them a lift…

Hedgerows begin to rise and luxuriant vegetation closes in. The road twists and winds past the entrance to Greenway down towards the river, offering glimpses of the village of Dittisham through the towering beeches.

And then – there you are, on the quay, the ferryman's cottage rising behind you with its thatched roof and smoking chimneys; to your left across the river, Viper's Point; straight ahead the village of 'Gitcham'.

And most special of all – and it's an odd sensation in today's hectic, fraught, traffic-ridden world – an almost tangible, still silence.

(Left) Galmpton pool with morning mist

(Right) Galmpton pool

(Left) The Greenway ferry bell

(Right) The ferryman's cottage

Dittisham from Greenway

Perhaps for this reason, it is with a strange feeling almost of trepidation that I ring the bell to summon the ferry.

In the quietly evocative opening to *Ordeal by Innocence*, Arthur Calgary, the Antarctic explorer, comes to the river at dusk, and is left by his driver to cross his rubicon alone. He brings information which will change his life and the lives of the rest of the cast in the novel for ever. He too has suffered a strange bout of amnesia, an echo of a similar occurrence in Agatha Christie's life.

There has been a ferry at this point since Bronze and Iron Age times. It formed part of a trading route from Halwell, the most important settlement in the area before the advent of Totnes, through to Galmpton and on to Churston Cove. Greenway was originally Greyn Way – the grain way. In more recent times the ferry was used to transport horses and donkeys to the Galmpton Tuesday market.

DITTISHAM AND GALMPTON

(Left) *The ferry*

(Right) *Ferryman*

The four pence that Calgary pays the ferryman has now, with inflation, risen to one pound fifty. Dittisham has also changed. The second-home phenomenon has hit here too. Gone are the days when the houses which represented the foreground of the village were principally in the refreshment line, and tea with cockles or shrimps could be had for any number at short notice. Gone are the days when up to six paddle-steamers at a time would line up either side of the wooden pier and disgorge their cargo of day-trippers.

Now, the ferryman informs me, Fisherman's Cottage, which was used by the Mallowan family when the American navy requisitioned Greenway House during the Second World War, has been recently valued at 1.7 million pounds. If house prices in Galmpton have risen, then here they have gone through the roof, so to speak. Mere common mortals need oxygen just to talk about prices at these stratospheric levels. The fact of the matter is, unless you are a well-known TV presenter, greetings card mogul or of some similar such ilk, don't even think about moving in here.

Stepping off the ferry one finds oneself in front of the Ferry Boat Inn. It is outside this pub – The Three Dogs in the novel *Dead Man's Folly* – that Mordell, the half-blind, nonagenarian ferryman comes to grief one dark, cloudy night after imbibing three pints of ale. A beery stumble on the quay and his body is washed up at Helmouth the next day. .

The board outside the pub informs that it will open at around noon (approximately). A quick visit to ask directions and then we continue up the hill. Chocolate-box cottages, fronted by flowers, line the ascent. Curiosity

The Ferry Boat Inn

(Left) Flowers outside a cottage

(Right) A cottage window

is too strong and you are drawn to nosily peek into windows – Fisherman's Cottage, Plum Tree Cottage. Designer kitchens, top-of-the-range Welsh slate floor slabs. These are the windows from which Calgary felt watched as he made his way to his appointment at Viper's Point. How things have changed. I do, of course, speak out of pure, unadulterated envy.

The hill levels out at the street appropriately named The Level. The road to the right leads up to the church and The Red Lion pub which gets the briefest of name checks in a character's alibi in *Ordeal by Innocence*. The lane to the left leads gently up to the Old Rectory, home of the Lords of the Manor of Dittisham. From here the track then climbs sharply upwards to the right. Looking back one has a marvellous view over Dittisham lake and further on to Torbay.

On this expanse of the river during the 1560s one might have come across three of Britain's greatest seafarers learning their craft: Humphrey Gilbert, Walter Raleigh and John Davis. Davis was born at Sandridge, the Italianate villa, just upstream from here, Gilbert and Raleigh at Greenway. The latter two would also go on to have chequered political careers as we saw in the chapter on Dartmouth. Davis, however, was totally focused on the sea and is generally acknowledged as one of the greatest navigators of his age. He penned two nautical treatises and invented a new double quadrant and backstaff, called Davis' quadrant. His all-consuming goal at this point in his life was to discover, by sailing up the west coast of Greenland, a North West passage to Cathay (China) and the Land of Spices. After several voyages, he arrived in 1587 as far as 72 degrees 46 minutes north – near to present day Upernavik – tantalisingly close to the true North West Passage… but then was blocked by ice.

The map still reveals today the path he took through these frozen wastes: place names like Exeter Sound, Totnes Road and Cape Chudleigh.

I think back to a book I once read about the construction of the great cathedrals in Europe which underlined how difficult it is nowadays to imagine the immense feeling of awe that people at that time, living in wooden houses, would have felt, seeing these medieval twin towers soaring skywards. Likewise, it is hard for us now to appreciate what places like the Dart must have seemed like then for the common man hearing the tales of

The Old Rectory

sailors returning from voyages to strange and unknown worlds. This was, for your average Elizabethan, the sixteenth century equivalent of Cape Canaveral

The path, in the meantime, has led us up to Fire Beacon hill at over 160 metres above the river. This was one of the beacons set up all along the south coast to warn of the sighting of a Spanish invasion force. Humphrey Gilbert had written in 1577, 'A discourse how her Majesty may annoy the King of Spain'. In 1588, right on cue, the Spanish, considerably more than irked by England's expansionist policies in the New World and the persistent attacks by privateers on their treasure ships, launched their famous Armada. This put a stop to Davis' exploration as he was recalled for defensive duty. Unfortunately, no sooner had the Armada been defeated, than his main North West Passage sponsor died. His next voyage was to be an attempt to reach the Pacific through the straits of Magellan. Ill-fated from the start it became a succession of mutinies, desertions, disease and disastrous weather. Small consolation, amidst all this, he discovered the Falkland Islands. Worse was to come. On his return, he found his wife had taken up with another man. From that moment on, he would embark on voyage after voyage to the Spice Islands of the East Indies, and though he became easily rich enough to retire he would never settle again. He ended up being killed during one of these voyages by Japanese pirates off the coast of Sumatra.

Back to the present. It's all downhill on the way back and there's time for a leisurely pint of that broadside ale I noticed on the way up. One discovers the locals are as friendly and hospitable as everywhere else we have been. And the view is spectacular.

There be no rush for the ferry anyway – it'll come when I ring…

The descent towards the ferry

Rainbow, from the Ferry Boat Inn

22
SALCOMBE

Towards Zero

Salcombe is a town in the South Hams district of Devon (nothing to do with charcuterie – Sham means a village). It is the setting for *Towards Zero*.

Towards Zero, along with *Cards on the Table*, was one of Max Mallowan's favourite Agatha Christie books. He admired above all the deft treatment of human character. He points out that all the landmarks mentioned in the book are clearly discernible and recommends it as a place of pilgrimage for those who want to identify the locations of a most ingeniously planned murder. And it is one of her most fiendishly torturous and satisfying puzzles.

There is a series of novels written about Devon while Max was away in the Second World War, almost as if Agatha wished in his absence to conjure up happy moments they had spent together. These include: *And Then There Were None* (1939), *The Regatta Mystery* (1939), *Evil Under the Sun* (1941), *The Body in the Library* (1942), *Five Little Pigs* (1942) and *Towards Zero* (1944). From the above list, I would also hazard a guess that she had visited Burgh Island with Max just before war broke out.

The River Yealm

The plot of *Towards Zero* hinges on there being a river which has at its mouth high cliffs – a lover's leap. The story also needed a ferry crossing a narrow expanse of water. In addition a resort was required with establishments that would be sought out by the well-to-do. Add to these ingredients the occasional rotting fish and the dish was ready to serve. The estuary (ria for the purists) from Kingsbridge to Salcombe fitted the bill exactly. Indeed, it would seem that in this case it was the topography of the location that actually suggested the plot.

The book features a map at the beginning. Salt Creek corresponds to Salcombe. Saltington is Kingsbridge. East Portlemouth, on the opposite bank, where Edward Latimer lodged, has become Easterhead

(Left) Riverside residence, Kingsbridge

(Right) Between Kingsbridge and Salcombe

The river Yealm's new name is the River Tern. It is here on a boat in the final stages of the novel that Superintendent Battle, Hercule's star pupil, gives a masterly summing up (with a little help from behind the scenes) in his famous *Towards Zero* speech.

Gull's Point lies on the north side of South Sands though may have been suggested by Overbecks on the opposite side of the cove. Stark Head, the site of the thwarted suicide – is either Bolt Head or Sharp Tor – Agatha has simplified somewhat the contour of the coast. Balmoral Court is most probably based on the Marine Hotel which we know for certain Agatha stayed at during the war and most probably before that, too. (The hotel swallowed up the

View from Overbecks to Salcombe

(Left) View of Salcombe – Gull Point would have been on the hill to the left

(Right) View from Sharp Tor towards Prawle Point

original Ringrone House built in 1839, becoming the Marine Hotel in the 1890s). Torquay goes under the familiar alias of St Loo – it is here that Neville Strange loses his tennis final.

Agatha had done her homework on the area. Audrey and Thomas discuss the treacherous currents flowing over the Bar (a particularly insidious sand bank at the mouth of the river) especially on the ebb tide. In 1916 the Salcombe lifeboat (still merely an open rowing boat at that time) was turned stern over bow by a freak wave with the loss of 13 lives while trying to negotiate the entrance to the estuary.

As usual, Agatha delights in playing name games with readers who have some knowledge of the places involved. As we have said, the Balmoral, the 'decent old-fashioned hotel' where the unfortunate Mr Treves is staying is the Marine Hotel with which the author was familiar. Yet just before his arrival, Mr Treves is lamenting the demolition of the Marine Hotel in Leahead where he usually stays. There are in-jokes for 'family' readers, too. The same character at the end of dinner comments on how he much preferred the old-fashioned routine where ladies left the dining room when the port went round. Agatha, who was infuriated by this custom, went as far as having the billiard room ripped out at Greenway to stop male guests adjourning there for port and cigars after dinner, forcing them to converse with the ladies.

My homework also threw up some interesting facts.

Not surprisingly, the village at the outset was predominantly involved in fishing and its sister industry, smuggling. It was surprise to me, however, to find out that in the nineteenth century Salcombe was a major player in the fruit trade. Fruit was imported from Spain and the Mediterranean but also from the Azores and the Bahamas. Cargo included oranges, lemons, pineapples, coconuts and the mysterious shaddock. These last were a type of giant grapefruit named after the eponymous captain who first imported them from the West Indies.

Wood was also imported for shipbuilding. Most of the Victorian houses in the town date from this period and were built for shipowners or masters. Overbecks, home of the original batty inventor, Otto Overbecks, was started in 1901. Apart from his (apparently quite successful) electronic rejuvenator for defying the aging process, the house also contains his formidable collections of lucanidae, lepidoptera, and a taxidermal menagerie that once terrified a young friend of mine. The sub-tropical gardens have splendid views back up the estuary and across towards Prawle Point.

Fortunately, just about the time of the decline in the fruit trade and the advent of the iron steam ship, the fashion for sailing started to take off – led in great part by His Royal Highness The Prince of Wales. The Salcombe Yacht Club was founded in 1874.

Between the wars the town developed as a holiday resort and sailing really became popular. So much so that the Salcombe Sailing Club was founded in 1922. The yacht club, you see, was only for gentlemen – the sailing club for the common folk.

During the Second World War, as we progress through the book certain themes become familiar, Salcombe became an Advance Amphibious Base for the United States Navy. Many vessels of Force U sailed from here for Utah Beach, Normandy.

Since the war, tourism has taken over as the main source of income.

* * * * * *

The town gained some unwelcome publicity in 1975 which would surely have had Christie reaching for her notebook. The Marine Hotel at that time was managed by a certain, John Allen, womaniser, but married with two young children. On 26 May his wife, Patricia, and children vanished into thin air never to be seen again.

Circumstances regarding the disappearance were odd to say the least. The three left all their clothes, had no money, income or passports, and were never heard of again by relatives. Their car was found in a car park with two dinghy oars sticking out through a window. But there were no bodies. Police hit a dead end.

In 2002, following the publication of a book accusing him of the murder written by a disgruntled ex-lover, he was brought to trial. An even more incredible story came out. In 1967 John Angel had been married to another woman. He had staged a Reggie Perrin style life-changing suicide appearing to throw himself off Beachy Head. He then bigamously married his second wife, Patricia, eventually moving to Salcombe.

On 16 December 2002 at Exeter Crown Court, the jury found the defendant guilty of murder and he was sentenced to 18 years.

Agatha Christie – it was a recurring theme of many of her works – would certainly have approved of the fact that no matter how long had elapsed since the misdeed, justice was seen, finally, to have been done.

23
CHURSTON CHURCH AND COURT

The Good Shepherd

As a child, my grandfather would take me along the road from Windy Corner that snakes through the links golf course on its way to Brixham. We would look for, and occasionally catch (if we were quick enough), lizards basking on top of the stone walls that line the lane. You hardly ever see a lizard nowadays.

Today I seem to have got caught up in a massive road race. I find myself edging along at tortoise speed slowly creeping past a never-ending file of bobbing behinds, pleasant and not so pleasant by turns. There appear to be as many waving and directing race marshals as there are runners. In addition to runners, marshals and crawling automobiles we have the odd hiker, cyclist, dog-walker and spectator. At one particularly bad bottleneck, a horse and rider are pulled up at the junction waiting to join the flow. It's hilarious. It does give me a chance for one of my favourite pastimes: eyeing the real estate. Churston is a modern development of mainly rather twee bungalows with immaculately manicured gardens. Proximity to the golf ensures, of course, that prices remain in the upper brackets for the bay.

Churston church lies about a mile further down this road. The name Churston apparently comes from the saxon: *cyric tun* – 'town of the cross'. The remains of the cross around which the Saxon community would gather to worship is leaning against the wall of the porch of the church. Soon after 1066 a stone chapel was built for the Norman lord and his family. As the latter-day Lady of the Manor it was proper that Agatha Christie would attend services here when in residence at Greenway.

Across the fields, one sees a cluster of buildings. A church with next to it an inn. The classic heart of an English village. I think I would be correct in saying that these days most people making their way along here are more likely bound for the latter rather than the former.

The Churston Court's brochure tells us it is a Grade I listed Saxon Manor House which opened as an inn during the reign of Elizabeth I and whose early locals used to include Humphrey Gilbert and Walter Raleigh (so maybe the first pub in the country to have a smokers' room?).

(Opposite) Churston village across the fields

AGATHA CHRISTIE'S DEVON

(Left) Churston Court

(Right) The main bar at the Churston Court

Meet the locals

Agatha Christie used to regularly pop in after services to lunch with Lord and Lady Churston. The cook of the time also recalled that Agatha would come into the kitchen afterwards and thank her for the wonderful meal. The claim that she was inspired here to write 'Death on the Links' [sic] is slightly dubious. To start with the book was published in 1923 long before she came to Greenway. Also *Murder on the Links* is set in France (Hercule Poirot makes his second appearance before the British public). Agatha Christie says herself the inspiration for this rather melodramatic work was a real-life French murder case – a 'cause celebre' where various people got murdered, one of them, somewhat gruesomely, with her own false teeth.

Melodramatic is a word that could also be applied to the décor of the pub, or inspired – it depends on your taste. It certainly is a labyrinth of rooms of varying shapes and sizes with sloping walls, skull-crunchingly low doorways, twisting corridors, suits of armour, worn sofas, candles and tapestries and it is doubtless full of secret passages, hidden panels, and inglenook fireplaces. I must say over the years I have come to like it.

Agatha Christie attended regularly the beautiful, little church next door. The autobiography tells us that, after many Sundays sitting looking at the plain glass window above the altar, she decided it would be nice to donate the proceeds of one of her books to the church to purchase a stained glass window. The conditions were that she should choose the artist, as she wished to avoid the reds and blues predominantly found in such works, and replace them with her favourite colours: mauve and pale green. The subject was to be of her choosing, too. Not the traditional crucifixion but the good shepherd holding a lamb – something the children would like. She got her way – and a jolly fine window, it is too.

The dining room at Churston Court

(Left) Churston Court and Church

(Right) St Mary the Virgin church

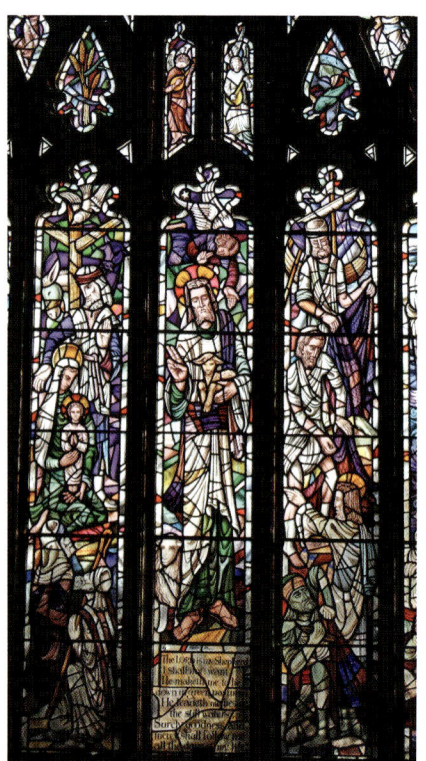

'The Good Shepherd'. Agatha's donated window at Churston

Laura Thompson identifies this donated story as *Greenshaw's Folly*, an embryonic version of a more well-known work. She also hints at a slightly more prosaic (cynical?) version of events. At this time Agatha was being pursued rather vigorously by the Inland Revenue for large amounts of tax which they reckoned were due to them, especially regarding her sales in America. One of the legal loopholes, one of the alleged ways of avoidance, was to gift works and their revenues to relatives: Mathew Prichard it is said had been given 'The Mousetrap', Rosalind would get the film sale of 'Witness for the Prosecution'. Now the Diocese of Exeter would benefit, too. Unfortunately, *Greenshaw's Folly* was a bit of a flop – apparently the Bishop of Exeter was non-too-pleased at the time.

The booklet sold at the church also states with, dare I say, a note of grievance that the Church authorities had had to 'sell back' the story to the literary agents for £1000, thus losing the permanent copyright.

Once lengthened and launched again as *Dead Man's Folly* it sold magnificently – a fact that must have rankled with the Bishop even more.

It's worth visiting during the Agatha Christie week in September – the floral arrangements are wonderful, the people always most friendly and welcoming.

Times change. Churches, like lizards, are also in decline. Most are closed if you try to visit: once-bitten-twice-shy victims of theft and vandalism. The churches mentioned in this book are making a valiant attempt to continue to fulfil their function of yesteryear in our rapidly evolving society. They prove that, at least for some, the church is still the stalwart to town and village life that it was in the past.

(Left) Flowers in a niche

(Centre) Rose in churchyard

(Right) In the week of the Flower Festival

24
BLACKPOOL SANDS

Drowsing in the Sun

Blackpool Sands is Devon's answer to 'The Beach'. It is the area's best kept secret – not that it's deserted, it never is, it's full of locals. But, we don't tell outsiders and as a local, myself, I really shouldn't be revealing this.

Without doubt, Blackpool Sands is one of the most beautiful beaches in the British Isles. The first glimpse you get is of a perfect crescent of yellow sand.

The first view of Blackpool Sands, arriving from Dartmouth

Blackpool Sands from the south – the 'black pool' is just out of picture bottom left.

An early postcard – notice the pool and the sea wall

The name always baffled me when I was a child – being as far from Blackpool as you could possibly imagine. Later, I found out that the name Black or Blag in Devonshire dialect means holy or sacred and for this reason was often applied to landmarks or boundaries. There is a pool and a stream flowing out to sea on one side of the beach. This stream marks the boundary between the parishes of Stoke Fleming and Blackawton. Hence the name Blackpool. Not all agree. The more prosaic version of the name is that on one side of the beach there is a black pool.

It's the most marvellous place to spend the day. There are excellent facilities, shop and licensed café. The setting is perfect – a golden sickle surrounded by dark wooded cliffs. My only gripe would be the icy water. Whatever the sun is doing, it is always freezing.

There are many photos of the Christie, I should say the Mallowan family, picnicking on the sands. There can be no doubt that the spot was in her mind as, at the very end of the autobiography, she thought back over her full life. She makes a list of the things she can no longer do as she grows older. I have the suspicion that she loved lists – there would have been lists for shopping, lists of things to do, lists of possible books, lists of ideas. Anyway, there at the top of this list, and preceded by a weighty 'alas', is swimming in the sea. Closing the list is the one thing she is still able to enjoy, 'sitting in the sun, gently dropping off'.

Many times researching this book there have been places where you are acutely aware of what has been there before you. You stand, trying to imagine, to absorb, what it must have been like, how it would feel to be transported back in time. On the spot where Ashfield must have stood, I waited to see the little girl with the hoop. On Burgh Island you are aware that Edward VIII, Noel Coward or Churchill even Poirot might have been sitting in the exact spot where you are now. It's even more strange when you know something violent has happened or that people have died. During the Hundred Years War, a French invasion force landed at Slapton with the intention of marching on Dartmouth. Six hundred years ago Blackpool sands was topographically similar to Slapton with a retaining beach backed up by marshes and reeds. The English decided to wait for them on the other side of the marsh on the high ground below Stoke Fleming. The French had been separated and lost contact with their archers. Prudence would have suggested regrouping and waiting for the bowmen to catch up. However, some competitive bravado between rival factions meant that they launched an assault immediately. Under a shower of English arrows the French were massacred…

The beach's eventful past did not stop there. As on most secluded coves in the area, smuggling was a popular activity. There are the usual rumours of tunnels running here and there. There were wrecks. Your

BLACKPOOL SANDS

From the Captain's Seat

Hydrangea, Blackpool Gardens

money or your life, stand and deliver, was pronounced here for the last time on British soil in 1873. More recently, the Americans practised their D Day landing techniques here as at Slapton, The concrete blocks of the car park are US army surplus purchased after the war by Sir Ralph Newman

The Newman family has owned the beach since 1790. It's now a thriving business with the shop and the café. The family made their fortune with the triangular commerce: salt, dried cod, port wine, described in the chapter on Dartmouth.

On the other side of the road there is an even better kept secret than the beach itself. A door in the wall leads to a hidden garden. It was started in 1896 by Robert Lydston Newman as a collection of semi-tropical specimen plants from all over the world. My favourites are, in fact, the oldest – the Monterey Pine on the first bend and the magnificently textured cork oaks on the lowest path. Built on a series of terraces, it zigs in wide zags to the highest point – the Captain's Seat which affords a marvellous view over the throng of beach-revellers towards Start Point. There's a feeling I experienced at Greenway looking down to the crowded river – the feeling of being in a deserted wonderful place just yards from the massed holiday traffic. I wander back down towards the road.

A deep breath, the door opens, and you are back in the real world.

APPENDICES

1. Agatha Christie's life

Agatha Christie was born on 15 September 1890 in a Victorian villa – Ashfield – on Barton Road in the Tormohun (Torre) area of Torquay. Barton at that time was on the edge of the town, almost in the countryside – not as fashionable as the Warberries or Meadfoot but still a neighbourhood for well-to-do families as can be seen from the many villas still remaining in the area. Eden Phillpotts, the then famous novelist, for example, lived just down the road at Oakhill.

Agatha's childhood, as recounted in the autobiography, was particularly happy. She doted on her father, Frederic Miller, an American whose profession on the register of baptisms in All Saints Church is described as 'Gentleman'. He passed his life between the Royal Yacht Club down at the harbour and Torquay cricket ground. The family had three servants: a cook, housemaid and parlourmaid, and were comfortably off.

She did not attend school – her mother, Clarissa, choosing to educate her at home. Her main interests as a child were dancing, the piano, rollerskating and swimming.

Her father died when she was 11 and the family were forced to make economies for the first time. She writes in the autobiography of how, for instance, the once lavish dinner menus became more frugal – things were never quite the same again.

In 1912, she met Archibald Christie, a strikingly handsome RFC officer, at a dance at Ugbrooke House, near Exeter. They married on Christmas Eve 1914 (with Agatha telling her mother only after the event) and spent their honeymoon (all one night of it) at the Grand Hotel in Torquay. The next day Archie returned to the front.

As a volunteer nurse, she soon found herself working in the dispensary at Torquay Hospital where she became familiar with poisons and started writing in quieter moments her first novel: *The Mysterious Affair at Styles*.

After the war, as a young wife and mother – her daughter Rosalind was born on August 5 1919 – the family moved to London.

She had become intensely attached to her mother after the death of her father and was devastated when she died in 1926. She moved back to Ashfield temporarily to sort out the house, her mother's belongings and the estate. Weeks later Archie's odd behaviour during this period was explained when he arrived from London and said he wanted a divorce.

Her mother dead, her dream of a life spent with the man she loved in pieces – these were truly heartbreaking blows for such a very private, shy person. She was unable to cope. She found herself in the full glare of public scrutiny after the bizarre episode of her disappearance and the eleven days spent in the Hydro Hotel in Harrogate, where she was subsequently discovered using a false name. Her broken marriage was laid out publicly for all to see—it must have seemed like a living hell for one so sensitive.

To get away from it all, she took the Orient Express to the Middle East and ended up in Baghdad. Here she met the young archaeologist and Oxford graduate, Max Mallowan, 13 years her junior. Eventually she gave in to his insisting, married him and set up home in Oxfordshire. This was a marriage not solely but much more of minds than her first – the couple worked together on digs extensively in the Middle East, with Agatha becoming quite a proficient archaeologist. Their union, quite different from the first marriage to Archie, allowed her wounded emotional psyche to heal – she found peace of mind and companionship – and left her free to concentrate on her main passion – her work. Her output from this moment on was truly remarkable.

In 1938, she sold Ashfield – houses had sprung up around it and it was no longer the idyllic location on the edge of the Devon countryside – what's more, a new Grammar School now obscured the splendid views of the bay. She bought Greenway, a marvellous country house on the banks of the Dart facing Dittisham – formerly the home to Sir Humphrey Gilbert, with magnificent gardens stretching along the river. This was to be her holiday residence for the rest of her life.

She never forgot Ashfield – a room was created at Greenway which housed pictures and furniture from the old house she had grown up in and which held so many of her beloved childhood memories. In 1962, she heard that there were plans to bulldoze Ashfield and build flats on the site. Appalled, she offered to buy the house back and turn it into an old folks home. But there was no stopping the development. In one of the most colossal lacks of foresight ever perpetrated by a local council, Torquay town planners allowed the demolition to proceed, and Ashfield was no more. Amazing – as Agatha Christie was, even at that time, the most famous woman novelist in the world; she had by then written 62 of her 81 novels and 'The Mousetrap' had been running for ten years non-stop at that point.

Agatha Christie died at her home in Wallingford on January 14 1976.

2. Agatha Christie's craft

Detractors of Agatha Christie have often criticised the lack of 'depth' of her characters. To do so is to totally miss the point. Her books are like puzzles. The reader is there to find the solution to the mystery. Like Poirot or Marple, he, himself, becomes a detective and is invited to pit his wits against the author – to distinguish red herrings from real clues (always having to bear in mind that even the reddest of herrings might actually contain the solution).

To do this one reads actively, not passively. Characters are not 'given' – they are sketched out on the page – readers are left to fill in the rest. That is not to say that they are cardboard cut-outs. Very often motives for crimes are psychological and so necessarily we will have to know key facts about characters. Let us not forget, either, that Agatha Christie is a master of dialogue – witness her stage successes. She is an expert at creating personalities with a minimum of conversational exchanges.

It's very much like the real world where we often called upon to judge from appearances and from what people say. And how often do we learn, as we do in the novels, that we can't always take what someone says or how they appear at face value?

The reader comes to realise that he is dealing with only one character in one setting – Agatha Christie, herself, in her study. Reader and author, like two chess players, engage in combat, each trying to outwit the other. The reader knows he is not being asked to believe or identify with the characters – the only character he need concern himself with is Agatha Christie herself.

Similar criticisms have been made regarding the omission of detailed description of places, locations or settings in the books.

There are many possible reasons for this. The first being, perhaps, that her mother when she used to read to her as a child used to skip the 'boring' descriptions in Walter Scott and Dickens!

Another possible reason might be a sort of uneasiness or embarrassment when describing things too close to home. She was always a very private person, and this reserve carried over into her novels. She clearly loved Devon, Torquay, Dartmoor and the South Hams, yet the rare descriptions of these places are always rather stilted and conventional. Was it that when describing places that she personally found enchanting she perhaps experienced the same awkwardness as Franklin Clarke when he describes the idyllic little beach with sparkling white stones, deep green trees and sapphire blue water at Elbury Cove in *The ABC Murders*? (Though Franklin may also have other issues…).

This said, however, perhaps we should look, rather than at her shyness or maternal influences, more at her style of writing. It follows logically from what we have said regarding character that, in an Agatha Christie novel, everything superfluous to the plot, that is, to the conundrum that the reader is presented with, is pared down to an absolute minimum. Token 'real' place names are given, but altered in such a way as to keep the reader aware of the fictitious nature of the account (they always seem to sound slightly ridiculous – for example, St Loo, Helmouth or Dillmouth)

Christie has no qualms whatsoever in adapting real places to her own literary purposes. An example of this is *And Then There Were None*. The inspiration for the location is clearly Burgh Island but Christie had several pre-requisites for the plot to function.

The key to the whole novel is isolation – to this end the island is moved a mile offshore. Next, the hotel is switched to the seaward-facing side so that the village on the mainland is not visible to the guests. All that was then needed was bad weather – it duly arrives – to seal the victims' inescapable destiny.

If we do get a physical description of place or character: Mr So and So's got a beard, it's snowing, bees are buzzing, the description of the topography of a river – then the reader's ears should prick up – something is definitely afoot. Description is only ever there for the specific purposes of the plot.

For example, *The Sittaford Mystery* hinges on there being an expanse of moor prone to heavy snowfalls and the consequent difficulty of moving between quite distant snow-bound locations in a very short time in order to perpetrate a murder. This, and only this, is what prompts the descriptions of the moorland scenery.

Another example is *Zero Hour* whose intricate plot was suggested by, and would not work without, the particularities of the geographical location.

The need for description of location to interconnect with plot can also produce some bizarre descriptive effects, as in a passage from *Peril At End House* where the vigorous, pleasant humming of bees in the hotel garden is underlined with a little too much insistence. The reason becomes clear a few pages later when the heroine, sitting in the sun outside the hotel, instinctively jerks her head back to avoid a passing wasp – she has a long-standing fear of bees and wasps – a wasp which later turns out to have been a bullet whistling through her hat, the third attempt on her life in as many days.

These are clearly not novels designed to create an illusion of reality. The reader does not judge them as such – but rather as marvels of pure literary ingenuity. As Gilbert Adair points out, this totally antithetical approach to the classic nineteenth century novel makes them in a certain sense very modern, even 'Modernist' novels.

Paradoxically, Agatha Christie, the author of books bought traditionally at stations and airports to kill a few hours en route to one's destination, has today become the doyenne of the some of the most respected of contemporary French intellectuals such as Michel Houellebecq and Pierre Bayard. This would undoubtedly have made her smile.

Novels referred to and the chapters in which they appear

The Mysterious Affair at Styles (1920) 11, 12; *Murder on the Links* (1923) 23; *The Man in the Brown Suit* (1924) 13; *Partners in Crime* (1929) 9; *The Sittaford Mystery* (1931) 14; *Peril At End House* (1932) 15; *Why Didn't They Ask Evans?* (1934) 7; *Parker Pyne Investigates* (1934) 12; *Three Act Tragedy* (1935) 3; *The ABC Murders* (1936) 16, 17, 18; *Hercule Poirot's Christmas* (1938) 11; *And Then There Were None* (1939) 19; *Evil Under the Sun* (1941) 19; *The Body in the Library* (1942) 15; *Five Little Pigs* (1942) 1; *Towards Zero* (1944) 22; *Come Tell Me How You Live* (1946) 16; 'The Mousetrap' (1952) 13; *Hickory Dickory Dock* (1955) 12; *Dead Man's Folly* (1956) 1, 16, 20, 21, 23; *4.50 from Paddington* (1957) 16; *Ordeal by Innocence* (1958) 20, 21; *The Pale Horse* (1961) 9, 11; *Postern of Fate* (1973) 2, 10; *Sleeping Murder* (1976) 6, 15; *The Problem at Pollensa Bay – The Regatta Mystery* (1992) 20.

Acknowledgements

Special thanks for help in producing this book go to: Simon Butler and Sharon O'Inn (Halsgrove), Nick Haworth, Robyn Browne, (Greenway); Janet Cooper,(Torquay Library); Hilary White and the people at All Saints; Filippo; Bob Farquhar (personal trainer); Steve Bonnet, (technical support); Nirosha Holton, (The Grand Hotel); David St. John-Scott, (Midas Constructions); Ray Nickells, (postcards); Fred Payne (Torquay Hospital); Keith Clarke, (The Moorland Hotel); James Hull, (Kents Cavern); Jean Reid, Geoff Old, Barry Chandler, (Torquay Museum); Yvonne Widger, (Dartington Hall Trust Archives); Pete Hamill (The Tavistock Inn); Deborah Clarke and staff, (Burgh Island); All the guys at Greenway Ferry Service; the staff at Churston Court; the people at Churston Ferrers Church; my family at the Devon School of English for spurring me on to give it my best shot; sister, Nicky; Nick, Liberty, Bella & Betsy for their patience and support and, of course, Rachel. The following images are used by kind permission: P. 9 – Greenway House, The National Trust Photo Library; P. 17 – Greenway Library, The National Trust Photo Library; P. 19 – The Herald Express; P. 21 – Map, Torquay Library; P. 58 – The Torquay Times, Torquay Library; P. 63 – Agatha Christie Suite, The Grand Hotel; P. 67 – The Dispensary, Fred Payne; P. 77 – The Donkey, Kents Cavern; P. 78 –The Rocky Chamber, Kents Cavern; P. 79 – Publicity shot, Kents Cavern; P. 112 – The Mermaid Suite, Deborah Clarke, Burgh Island Hotel.